# CELEBRITIES, AND EXPERTS APPLAUD
## SAVE THE ANIMALS!

★

"Unusually fair and clear-minded. If we all follow her reasonable, well-considered suggestions, we will soon see the end of cruelty to our fellow creatures."
**—Rue McClanahan, co-star of "The Golden Girls"**

"A quick and easy read! Full of solutions for how to save animals from unnecessary suffering . . . and that includes homo sapiens."
**—River Phoenix, actor**

"Contains information that will help make life healthier, happier and more generally fulfilling for my gentle, loving, and snuggly catfriend, Frida. It will also mean better lives for all her relatives and mine."
**—Alice Walker, author of *The Color Purple***

"This is a 'why-to,' 'how-to' guide for anybody who wants to get involved, at whatever level they're comfortable with."
**—Paul Obis, publisher and editor in chief, *Vegetarian Times***

"A brave and wonderful book. Ingrid Newkirk has surrounded and zeroed in on virtually every field of cruelty to our fellow creatures."
**—Cleveland Amory author of *The Cat Who Came for Christmas* and president of the Fund for Animals and NEAVS**

"Gently, persuasively, Newkirk offers the reader antidotes to the pain—concrete suggestions to help them become animal-conscious consumers. Truly, a book of social significance."
**—Cesar Chavez, human rights activist and president of the United Farm Workers**

"PETA has done great work in clarifying our relationship and responsibility to animals, and by extension, the rest of the planet."
**—Peter Max, artist**

"Exciting ideas and innovative approaches to what will clearly be the movement of the 1990s."

**—Tony La Russa, manager, Oakland A's**

"This book gives you so many ways to be of assistance to our animal friends. Everyone can find at least one more way to be involved and make a difference."

**—Sally Struthers, actress**

"Somewhere up the road we will learn to embrace all creatures with kindness. Ingrid Newkirk's book will help."

**—Paul Harvey**
**nationally syndicated radio commentator**

"An indispensable guidebook to the survival of the animals and the planet itself."

**—Bobbie Ann Mason, author of *In Country***

"A rare gem."

**—Colman McCarthy**
**nationally syndicated *Washington Post* columnist**

"A must for every activist. Don't leave home without it."

**—Tom Regan**
**author of *The Case for Animal Rights* and**
**president of the Culture and Animals Foundation**

"Practical, comprehensive, educational, and—most of all—empowering."

**—Kim Bartlett, editor, *The Animals' Agenda***

"Will mitigate the suffering of millions. This is the book the animals have been waiting for."

**—Laura A. Moretti, editor in chief, *Animals' Voice Magazine***

"Gives people at all levels of involvement information to make their lives brighter and more compassionate."

**—John Robbins, author of *Diet for a New America* and**
**president of EarthSave**

"I've started practicing many of the suggestions in the book and already Opus is looking at me with a modicum of respect, thank God. I suspect, however, that he's wondering why they left off chapter 51: 'No Spanking! Housebreak Your Penguin with Financial Incentives.' "

**—Berke Breathed, author and illustrator of Bloom County and**
**Outland comic strips**

# SAVE THE ANIMALS!

## 101 EASY THINGS YOU CAN DO

INGRID NEWKIRK

**National Director, People for the Ethical Treatment of Animals (PETA)**

WARNER BOOKS

A Time Warner Company

To the memory of Ms. Bea, an old mixed-breed dog who died in 1986. The world had not treated her kindly in puppyhood, and when she left, a piece of my heart went with her.

I now know that *every* animal is someone's Ms. Bea or simply a Ms. Bea no one got to know.

The information contained in this book regarding products
that are tested on animals is accurate as of July 9, 1990.

Copyright © 1990 by Ingrid Newkirk
All rights reserved.
Warner Books, Inc., 666 Fifth Avenue, New York, NY 10103
Ⓦ A Time Warner Company

Printed in the United States of America
First Printing: October 1990
10  9  8  7  6  5  4  3  2  1

**Library of Congress Cataloging-in-Publication Data**

Newkirk, Ingrid.
    Save the animals!: 101 easy things you can do / Ingrid Newkirk.
        p.   cm.
    ISBN 0-446-39234-0
    1. Animal welfare.   I. Title.
HV4708.N49   1990
179'3—dc20                                            90-39197
                                                         CIP

*Book design: Giorgetta Bell McRee*
*Cover illustration: Berke Breathed*
*Cover Design: Anne Twomey*

The text of this book was printed on recycled paper.

# ACKNOWLEDGMENTS

Thanks for their invaluable contributions to this book go, first and foremost, to Kym Boyman, who became my special assistant only days before the book was a "go," who learned immediately how monumental a job she had accepted and threw herself generously and more than ably to the task; to the ever-efficient Vicky Kaempf, who smoothed the wrinkles out of every working day; to the talented PETA correspondents Christine Jackson, Teresa Gibbs, Carla and Karin Bennett, and Jill Leonard; to David Cantor for finding just the right quotes; to Karen Porreca, our meticulous librarian; to Alex Pacheco, for being my friend and inspiration; and to the tremendous team of activists who make up the PETA staff and who have personally "animal tested" everything you will find on these pages.

# CONTENTS

# FOREWORD

A long time ago we realized that anyone who cares about the Earth—really cares—must stop eating animals. The more we read about deforestation, water pollution, and topsoil erosion, the stronger that realization becomes. Of course, anyone who cares about *animals* must stop eating animals. Just the thought of what happens in a slaughterhouse is enough. We stopped eating meat the day we happened to look out our window during Sunday lunch and saw our young lambs playing happily, as kittens do, in the fields. Eating bits of them suddenly made no sense. In fact, it was revolting. If you want to live a longer and healthier life, the conclusion is exactly the same, *naturally*.

Ingrid Newkirk believes this, too, with all her heart. Her book is so chock full of insights into animals' lives and needs, as well as quick facts about everything from vegetarianism to making life more pleasant for your dog or cat, that you can't help but ask why this book hasn't come along sooner. The subtitle says ''101 Easy Things . . .'' but that's an understatement. This small book is full of tips on creative, interesting, tangible, and painless ways to be a powerful advocate for almost every kind of other-than-human being. Whether you are a musician, a carpenter, a nurse, a student, a homemaker, or even a farmer, there are suggestions that are custom written for you and can be implemented right away.

So, thanks from us, from PETA, and from the animals for caring enough to make a *big* difference. Happy reading!

LINDA MCCARTNEY

# INTRODUCTION

Ingrid Newkirk has written a brave and wonderful book. She has surrounded and zeroed in on virtually every field of cruelty to our fellow creatures, and, when it comes to the perpetrators, she takes no prisoners.

With it all, she has maintained her special brand of humor, one which in my capacity as president of the Fund for Animals and also of the New England Anti-Vivisection Society (NEAVS) I have come to know, both personally and professionally, is such a vital part of her. Who but Ingrid, for example, would have chosen chapter titles like "Mind Your Bees and Shrews," "Deer Editor," "Be Fish Friendly," "Winners Don't Eat Weiners," and "Silver Scream."

Her quotations are ones you won't soon forget. Take Gandhi's, for one—"I hold that, the more helpless a creature, the more entitled it is to protection by man from the cruelty of man." Or, for another, John Bryant—"There are three prerequisites for angling—a hook, a line, and a stinker."

"Never, never, never," she writes, "buy a caged bird." And she has, for rats, "Rat Facts," i.e., "Number of reported cases of humans bitten by rats in New York City in 1985: 311. Number reported bitten by other people: 1,519."

And "rat facts" aren't the only facts you'll learn here. Try lobsters:

> Lobsters are fascinating creatures. They have a long childhood, and an awkward adolescence. They use complicated signals to explore and establish social relationships with others. Their communications are direct and sophisticated. They flirt. Their pregnancies last nine

months. Some are right-handed, some are left-handed. They've even been seen walking hand-in-hand! Some can live to be more than 150 years old . . .

Many of her statements will shock you. They should. "See meat for what it really is," she writes, "antibiotic and pesticide-laden, rotting parts of a tortured animal." "Alligators and snakes," she writes again, "are usually conscious when skinned to make shoes, handbags and belts because no one can be bothered or wants to incur the extra expense of stunning them . . ." "Young Karakul goats are boiled alive by shepherds to produce 'kid' gloves because it tenderizes their skin."

Whether you can do anything about these things is up to you. Ingrid will show you how. But here too you will find simple advice every one of us can follow every day—"Turn that television off and resolve to walk and play daily with your faithful companion animal."

She calls this, typically, "Quality Time." So, too, is time spent with this extraordinary book.

—CLEVELAND AMORY

# PREFACE

In 1980, I helped found People for the Ethical Treatment of Animals (PETA). It happened because of a young political science student named Alex Pacheco who walked into the Washington, D.C., animal shelter one day and volunteered his services. As the beleaguered person in charge, I gladly put him to work.

It turned out that only a few months earlier, Alex had been aboard the Fund for Animals' ship, *Sea Shepherd*. The vessel's captain, Paul Watson, had recruited the first group of marine mammal "warriors," Alex among them, to hunt down a pirate whaling ship called the *Sierra*. Over the years, the *Sierra* had been responsible for butchering hundreds of whales in international waters. After combing the Atlantic, Watson and the crew of the *Sea Shepherd* found the boat off the coast of Portugal. They trailed it from a distance until it berthed in Lisbon, and when its crew was safely ashore, rammed its bow. The *Sierra* went to the bottom, never to harpoon another Great Blue again.

Alex had fled Portugal, overland, to England, where he met up with activists in the already well-established movement for animal rights. He learned how to interfere with foxhunters' cruel "sport" by mastering the hunting horn to call away hounds; marched in Trafalgar Square for the abolition of vivisection; and adopted a meatless diet of beans on toast and soy sausage rolls.

In his backpack, Alex carried copies of *Animal Liberation*, a book that had changed his way of thinking about animals. He lent it to me and, like tens of thousands of other people in the ten years that have passed since I read it, I came to realize as I turned the pages that, deep in my heart, I believed, along with Peter Singer, the book's author, that animals have a worth in and of themselves, and that they are not inferior to human beings but rather just different from us, and that they really don't exist for us nor do they belong to us. I also realized that it should not be a question simply of *how* they should be treated within the context of their usefulness, or perceived usefulness, to us, but rather whether we have a *right* to use them at all. Surely, as Henry Beston first stated and Singer reiterated: animals are "not our underlings, they are other nations caught with ourselves in the net of life and time."

Over the years, I had witnessed terrible cruelties. In my work as a humane officer, I had scraped dying animals from the roadways and crawled under buildings and in sewer pipes to retrieve what was left of little bodies ravaged by cars, disease, and human hands. I had held burned dogs in my arms; pulled starving horses, and even pigs, out of barns; and brought many a prosecution for willful acts of abuse. I had glimpsed behind the laboratory doors, where animal life is a cheap commodity and other-than-human beings are not uncommonly the victims of insensitivity, even sadism. Yet even I, a person who cares deeply for animals, had never considered that perhaps showing animals the little kindnesses, like a longer chain for the guard dog, a drink of water for the carriage horse, a painkiller for the guinea pig in the laboratory, or a hammerblow to the head to stun the steer at slaughter time, just wasn't enough. I hadn't realized that the greatest kindness was really to show enough respect for others to leave the animals in peace, unmolested.

I knew that while most people are appalled at the idea of cruelty to animals, few of them will ever see how a pig becomes a weiner, learn how raccoon mothers chew off their own feet in leghold traps to return to the babies left behind in their dens, or realize that rabbits have shampoo poured directly into their open eyes in crude tests. Like me, most people had only to be shown that such things are reality for billions of individual creatures to want to *do* something to stop the suffering.

The question was, WHAT could anyone do?

By forming PETA, Alex and I created an information hub. Through meetings, publications, and public events, we created the opportunity to show people exactly what animals endure in every human endeavor—from factory farming to cosmetics tests to circuses and zoos, hunting, and even that "peaceful" pastime, fishing. Most importantly, we felt that *knowing* the problem was only a first step and that the second step, *doing something to help*, has to be made as painless as possible in this convenience-oriented, rush-rush society.

Ten years ago, making a transition to vegetarianism, finding non-leather shoes, and choosing a lipstick that hadn't been tested on animals, was hard. There were few health-food stores, "cruelty-free" household products and cosmetics had to be made at home or ordered by mail, and no one publicly protested animal acts or sued their school for the right not to cut up the frog. Today, vegetarian cookbooks bend the bookstore shelves and, for those who hate to "give up" a food, there is a soy taste-alike for almost anything, from tofutti "ice cream" and "cheese" to tempeh burgers and tofu pups. Companies as large as Avon, Revlon, and Christian Dior Parfums have stopped hurting rabbits and other animals as part of their product testing and designers like Giorgio Armani and Bill Blass have stopped using fur. Mr. Armani has even had a label sewn inside his coats that reads, "Thank you, Giorgio, for saving our skins."

PETA has grown enormously. We now have more than 300,000 members throughout the United States, compassionate people who actively fight "institutionalized" animal abuse, no matter how cleverly disguised it may be behind advertising jingles, or how deeply ingrained it has become in our society. These people have switched from sloppy shoppers to caring consumers. They don't sit quietly when they know animals need their voices; they speak out. They don't accept cruelty; they fight it. Thanks to them, great changes are occurring, and the world is getting to be a better place for the other "animal nations" who share it with us.

This book can help you become one of those people. As you read it, you join a community of others who respect animals enough to make choices that affect them. Often these are simple choices, like which movie to see or which veterinarian or beauty salon to patronize. Sometimes, they're tougher ones, like what to do with your backyard or how to deal with your child's teacher's insistence that s/he dissect. You will learn how to make your vote count, how to influence magazine publishers and television producers with a few strokes of the pen. Your neighborhood stores will begin to reflect your choices by adding items to their shelves and perhaps even subtracting unacceptable ones, thanks to you.

If you only do a few of the things suggested in this book, you should feel good about yourself. The more you do, the better you'll feel, the happier your companion animals will be, the healthier you'll become, and the more impact you'll have on the world around you. Now, how can you beat that?

# THE UGLY SIDE OF BEAUTY

It is totally unconscionable to subject defenseless animals to mutilation and death, just so a company can be the first to market a new shade of nail polish or a new, improved laundry detergent. . . . It's cruel, it's brutal, it's inhumane, and most people don't want it.
>—**ABIGAIL "DEAR ABBY" VAN BUREN,** testifying before the House Judiciary Committee in support of the Consumer Products Safe Testing Act, March 1988

[I'm] a strong believer that it is important to campaign for products that use enlightened methods of testing.
>—**CANDICE BERGEN**

The worst sin towards our fellow creatures is not to hate them, but to be indifferent to them. That's the essence of inhumanity.
>—**GEORGE BERNARD SHAW,** Preface to *Doctor's Dilemma*

## BEAUTY ISN'T ONLY SKIN DEEP

Companies' slick advertisements of lipsticks, furniture polish, and other cosmetics and household products never include descriptions of what happens to the millions of rabbits, guinea pigs, and other animals still maimed and killed annually by many major companies in crude product tests.

The most common product tests are the Draize Eye Irritancy Test and the Lethal Dose 50 (percent) Test. The Draize test involves dripping

1

substances, such as nail polish and dandruff shampoo, into rabbits' eyes to study reactions (often bleeding ulcerations) during a 3-to-21-day testing period. Lethal Dose tests involve force-feeding substances, such as toilet bowl cleaner, to animals to observe reactions (including convulsions, emaciation, skin eruptions, and diarrhea) until a certain percentage, commonly 50 percent, of the animals die.

Don't be fooled by company claims that animal tests are required or that alternatives don't exist. *No* law mandates animal tests for cosmetics and household products—the tests are designed to limit the companies' liability to its customers in case of a lawsuit! Despite animal injuries and deaths in laboratories, hair dyes, bleaches, and drain cleaners may still poison and blind you if swallowed or poured into your eye. In 1987, 47,000 people were rushed to hospital emergency rooms in the U.S. with injuries resulting from contact with household products.

## THE SOLUTION

Never fear! More than 300 companies, including the Body Shop, Paul Mitchell, and Aveda, manufacture safe, gentle, effective products that are tested, not on animals, but through *in vitro* (test tube) studies, with sophisticated computer models, and on human skin (cloned or attached to volunteers!). Many companies are committed to using known-safe ingredients (there are now more than 600), rather than experiment with new chemical combinations.

- Write or call companies (e.g., L'Oréal and Procter & Gamble) to let them know that you will not be purchasing their products until they stop maiming animals in their product tests.
- Inform others. Most people aren't aware that their "cherry red" lipstick depends on animals suffering.
- Mobilize your community to encourage a company to go cruelty-free. Circulate a petition among your friends, family, neighbors, and school; collect products manufactured by the company; and send them in. This action may be "the straw that breaks the company's back," leading it to abandon cruel animal tests and declare a *permanent* ban.

## RESOURCES

- Choose from **PETA**'s Cruelty-free Shopping Guide. Write to **PETA,** P.O. Box 42516, Washington, DC 20015, for a wallet-size list of companies that do not test their products on other-than-human beings and those that do (also indicates which of the non-testing companies use animal-derived ingredients).
- Write to **Vegan Street** for its catalogue of "Cruelty-Free and Environmentally Safe Products," P.O. Box 5525, Rockville, MD 20855; 1-800-422-5525. It carries everything from soap and deodorant to non-leather hiking boots (perfect for hunt sabotages) and low-flow showerheads (perfect for afterwards!).

# 2 | CLEAN UP FOR THE ANIMALS

A man is truly ethical only when he obeys the compulsion to help all life which he is able to assist, and shrinks from injuring anything that lives.

—**ALBERT SCHWEITZER,** *The Philosophy of Civilization*

## THE PROBLEM

The approximately 5,200 pounds of trash generated by the average American family each year—accompanied by the massive amount of litter along highways, in forests, and in the oceans—makes the planet a mess. It not only clogs our waterways, it also strangles fishes, birds, and mammals. Every year, millions of other-than-humans are maimed and killed by our garbage and litter. Sometimes they push their faces into discarded food containers to lick them clean and get their heads stuck inside. Sometimes they swallow bits of indigestible plastic in the ocean that look like jellyfish. Our refuse can be injurious, even lethal.

## Chew on This

- The average American produces 1,300 pounds of trash in a year. There are 240 million Americans, so Americans produce 312 billion pounds of trash in a year. That's 54.8 million pounds *each day*.

4

- New York City's per-capita rate of garbage output is one-third higher than the national average and nearly twice that of Paris or Rome.
- Plastic trash dumped into oceans kills millions of beings each year. Plastic traps fish, mammals, turtles, and birds in knotted tangles, causing death by starvation, drowning, strangulation, or ingestion. The U.S. Academy of Sciences estimates 350 million pounds of packaging and fishing gear are lost or dumped by the commercial fishing industry each year.
- In July 1985, a dying one-year-old sperm whale washed ashore with a Mylar balloon lodged in his stomach.
- In September 1987, a half-ton leatherback turtle, disabled from a latex balloon and 3-foot ribbon blocking his pyloric valve, received a 3-foot gash from a propellor he was unable to dodge.
- Some experts estimate that plastic refuse kills more than 100,000 sea mammals and 2 million seabirds every year.
- The U.S. Office of Technology Assessment reports that the more than 20 million tons of plastic pollution produced each year pose a greater threat to marine mammals and birds than pesticides, oil spills, and contaminated run-off from the land.
- Approximately 14 billion pounds of trash are dumped into the sea every year.
- Plastic six-pack rings take 450 years to degrade. Birds who dive into the water to catch fish sometimes dive into and get strangled by these rings.
- Of the 190 pounds of plastic each U.S. citizen uses every year, about 60 pounds consist of packing thrown out immediately after a product is opened.
- Americans produce 154 million tons of garbage every year—approximately 50 percent of it is recyclable.
- Currently, only 5 percent of tin cans are recycled.

## THE SOLUTION

Always, the best advice is to consume less (to "live simply so that others may simply live"). But if we remain loyal to a consumer-oriented life-style, we should at least *carefully* dispose of everything we use and pick up after others who are not so careful. Here are a few pointers:

● Recognize that your garbage can be a trap—a potentially lethal picnic for animals in your neighborhood.

    • Avoid buying unnecessary plastic products. Buy juice in cardboard cartons, use wax paper instead of plastic wrap, and so on.

    • Recycle paper, aluminum, plastic, and glass. Call the **Environmental Defense Fund** hotline, 1-800-CALL-EDF, for the recycling center nearest you.

    • Tell grocery store managers that you prefer to buy products packaged in a nonpolluting, environmentally friendly way. Complain to the grocer if the produce department insists on shrink-wrapping items like cucumbers and tomatoes instead of selling them loose.

    • Rinse out jars and other containers in which animals' heads can get caught. Screw lids back onto empty jars before disposing of them, and put sharp tops and tabs inside of empty tin cans so they cannot slice tongues and throats.

    • Crush the open end of cans as flat as possible. The National Zoo drew protests when it used an elephant named Nancy to crush cans during Washington, D.C.'s Earth Day 1990 celebrations. There's a humane, everyday device that will do the job for you: "The Crusher!" It's available from **Pacific Fabrication,** P.O. Box 1008, Rancho Cucamonga, CA 91730; (714) 987-9371 (price $19.95).

    • Tear open one side of tough plastic and cardboard containers so that squirrels and other small animals cannot get caught in them. Many have died, unable to back out of inverted-pyramid yogurt cups.

    • Snip apart plastic six-pack rings, including the inner diamond. The rings are commonly found around the necks of wildlife ranging from turtles to water fowl. In a celebrated case in Maryland, Mary Beth Sweetland rescued a duck who, for months, had been ensnared in a plastic six-pack holder and was wasting away. Winning the duck's confidence took time. Mary Beth eventually lured him out of the water with cracked corn and, with a garden stake she had hidden up her sleeve, gently speared the plastic rings to the ground.

With a friend's help, she snipped the plastic (over which the duck's bill had begun to grow) and released the duck back to the lake.

• Use garbage cans with clasps, so young animals do not get caught in the bottom of them. Baby opossums and others fall in and cannot climb out.

If animals are tipping over your cans, store them in the garage or on an enclosed porch until trash collection day, or make a garbage-can rack from 2″ × 4″ lumber. One homeowner solved the strewn-garbage problem by tying a small bag of "healthful goodies" to the handle of his garbage can each night. Satisfied, the midnight raider leaves the garbage alone.

• Never dispose of razors and other dangerous items by dropping them in loose with your other garbage. One activist places used razor blades inside empty, rinsed-out and *sealed* cartons.

• Take care to clean up antifreeze spills carefully (and rinse out the rags you use to do so!); it is toxic, and animals are attracted to its sweet taste. Do not wash antifreeze down storm water grates. For more information about disposing of hazardous chemicals, call the **Environmental Protection Agency (EPA)** hotline: 1-800-424-9346 or (202) 382-3000.

• Carry your own string or canvas bags to the grocery store (cotton string bags are available from **Seventh Generation,** Colchester, VT 05446-1672; 1-800-456-1177) or, at least, choose paper bags over plastic. In the kitchen, use only biodegradable or photodegradable food storage bags, such as those available from **Earth Care Paper Co.,** 100 S. Baldwin Street, Dept. 4, Madison, WI 53703, and **Co-op America,** 2100 M Street NW, Suite 310, Washington, DC 20063.

● Join, create, or consider yourself the sole member of a beach brigade or park patrol.

• Pick up string, fishing line, and all plastic litter (bags, bottles, six-pack rings, lids, and disposable diapers) near streams and woods. Birds, turtles, dolphins, and even whales and otters can get tangled in or swallow such trash, and the result is injury and, often, even death.

• Beach clean-ups are usually held in the fall. For information on where and when one may be held near you, write **Coastal States**

**Organization,** c/o Margie Fleming, 444 N. Capitol St. NW, Suite 312, Washington, DC 20001; or, the **Center for Environmental Education,** 1725 DeSales Street NW, Washington, DC 20036.

• ... And, please, *never* launch helium balloons. Also, protest any balloon launches of which you might hear. When the balloons land, particularly in the water, they can be mistaken for food and cause whales, turtles, and other sea dwellers to choke and suffocate.

# 3 HOW SAD IS THAT DOGGIE IN THE WINDOW?

Whatever salespeople or sentimental books may state, WILD ANI-
MALS DO NOT MAKE GOOD PETS. Captivity, no matter how
"kind," is always cruel.

—JOAN WARD-HARRIS, *Creature Comforts*

We cannot glimpse the essential life of a caged animal, only the shadow
of [her] former beauty.

—JULIA ALLEN FIELD, "Reflections on the Death
of an Elephant," *Defenders* 42 (Spring 1967)

## THE PROBLEM

Raised without affection and stressed by shipping, animals found in pet
shops can suffer both physical and emotional problems that cause heart-
break, headaches, and behavioral problems for them and their human
companions as they grow. Humane officers can recount stories of pet
shop rejects and sick animals being drowned in the back room, left to
die, or shipped while ill or injured to cut costs.

### Puppy Mills Give Me Chills

While our shelters are bursting at the seams with unwanted animals
looking for good homes, pet shops encourage the irresponsible and
negligent proliferation of dogs and cats. About 360,000 puppies sold

in pet shops each year come from "puppy mills," breeding kennels
located mostly in midwestern states where "farmers" churn out
hundreds of yorkies, spaniels, poodles, and other pups in elevated,
outdoor cages, then ship them off like so many vegetables to market.
These places are notorious for their cramped, crude, and filthy conditions
and their continuous inbreeding of unhealthy and hard-to-socialize animals.

- The Humane Society of the United States estimates that more than
  one-half million puppies are produced annually to be sold almost
  exclusively to pet stores.
- Female dogs in puppy mill kennels are bred continuously, with no
  rest between heat cycles. They are killed when their bodies give
  out and they no longer can produce enough litters.
- The U.S. Department of Agriculture estimates that 25 percent of
  the 3,500 federally licensed breeding kennels operate under sub-
  standard conditions. As many as 1,600 kennels running without
  federal licenses are never inspected. A Humane Society of the
  United States' undercover investigation reported that 80 percent
  of 294 puppy mills examined had serious deficiencies, and that
  while 44 percent of the facilities inspected by the USDA in 1981
  had chronic and persistent deficiencies, the agency took no dis-
  ciplinary action.

## Exotic Exploitation

When you buy an exotic animal (an animal not native to this country)
from a pet shop, you may be unwittingly contributing to the cruel,
gruesome trade in lizards, birds, and snakes from Asia, South and
Central America, and Africa. Most of these usually colorful creatures
don't make it alive to the United States—it has been estimated that up
to ten birds die for one who makes it through the pet shop door, and
the ratio is similar for other species. Survivors are susceptible to premature death from stress, malnutrition, dehydration, improper handling,
illness, or general malaise. Most purchasers are unable or unwilling to
create a habitat that even remotely resembles that of exotics in their
natural homes.

- When birds are "legally" imported into the U.S., they must be inspected and quarantined. Thousands of birds arrive dead. Their deaths during transport are caused by inadequate perches and crating, temperature extremes, capture and transport shock, overcrowding, inadequate care and ventilation, disease, suffocation, unsanitary conditions, and lack of food and/or water. These stresses cause birds to peck and chew themselves and each other, resulting in severe injuries, including blindness. The Animal Welfare Act does not protect "cage birds."

- According to Clifford Warwick, consultant herpetologist for the People's Trust for Endangered Species, the pet trade has become a factor in the decline of the North American Box turtle; the demand for turtles as pets replaced that for Mediterranean tortoises when a 1984 law banned trade in the latter. Turtles are neglected and deprived of their needs during transport and before collection. They arrive at wholesalers dehydrated and thin, often dead. Like other reptiles, box turtles are very sensitive to climate changes, even within the United States; taking them to new locations as companions often kills them.

- Sixty percent of wild animals caught to be sold as exotic pets die before reaching their point of exportation.

## THE SOLUTION

- Resist buying "that doggy in the window"—the pet shop will just replace him or her using the profit you bring to their business. If you want to share your home with a dog or cat, visit your local pound or shelter. If you have the urge to possess animals who ordinarily live wild and free in their native lands, please think again. Living beings aren't toys or decorations, and wild animals should remain unfettered.

- Never buy animals as gifts, and tell others who may be in the market for a companion animal that there are many wonderful dogs and cats waiting at their local animal shelter. Leave leaflets outside your local pet shop during peak shopping times to educate potential buyers.

- Ask your city or county council members to pass an ordinance banning the sale and keeping of exotic wildlife except for rehabilitation purposes. Get a ban on the sale, painting, or coloring (including the ''harmless'' vegetable dyes) of chicks, bunnies, ducklings, and turtles. Fight permit applications for new pet shops unless they limit sales to supplies only.

## SOURCES

- Greta Nilsson's excellent book, *The Bird Business,* is available from the **Animal Welfare Institute,** P.O. Box 3650, Washington, DC 20007, for $5 postpaid.
- For more information on snakes, alligators, turtles, lizards, and crocodiles, contact the **Reptile Defense Fund,** 5025 Tulane Drive, Baton Rouge, LA 70808; (504) 767-6384.
- **PETA** has pamphlets on petshop-related subjects for you to distribute.

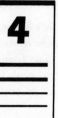

# 4 GIVE ANIMALS A VOICE

I am the voice of the voiceless;
    Through me the dumb shall speak,
Till the deaf world's ear be made to hear
    The wrongs of the wordless weak.

                . . .

And I am my brother's keeper,
    And I will fight his fight;
And speak the word for beast and bird
    Till the world shall set things right.

            —ELLA WHEELER WILCOX,
                1850–1919

Unseen they suffer
Unheard they cry . . .

## THE PROBLEM

Although other species have their own languages, we have yet to figure them out. Dolphins "click" up to 700 times a second and can reach frequencies 12 times higher than those audible to humans. Elephants communicate subsonically at frequencies too low for us to hear, rats at frequencies too high. Crows in the south of France have dialects that puzzle (and are probably the brunt of jokes for) crows in the northern wine country. Chimpanzees can use American sign language: Washoe, a twenty-five-year-old chimpanzee considered "family" by primatologist Roger Fouts, knows signs and, unaided, has taught her adopted son, Loulis, more than seventy of them. Chimpanzees do not have vocal chord configurations that would permit them to make the same sounds humans make. Most oppressed groups of human beings can speak for themselves; but until we learn to understand the languages of other-than-humans, we must "speak for the animals."

## THE SOLUTION

- Speak out! Within earshot of the shopper ahead of you at the check-out line, converse with a friend about that television special you saw on slaughterhouses. Have polite conversations, even with strangers, about the cruelty of fur and meat production—saying you just read a disturbing article is a good starter—particularly on public transportation, in dentists' and doctors' offices, or anywhere there's an audience. Also, help meat consumers by telling them what our government hasn't got around to yet: "Warning: This Product Causes Heart Attacks, Cancer, and Other Fatal Diseases" (1).*

- Deliver a televised free-speech message, often called "speak-outs." Adam Locke, a San Mateo, California, high school student, taped a spot concerning students' right to refuse to dissect animals. It was aired on five television channels and one radio station.

- If you have a group, try a public service announcement (PSA) on radio or TV. PSA's are ten- to sixty-second notices that stations are required to air by the Federal Communications Commission in order to balance the effect of paid advertisements and present balanced coverage of issues. They are free to nonprofit community groups, but you may need professional help getting one done. Possible topics include the importance of giving companion animals love and attention, and of not leaving dogs in cars on warm and hot days.

- Participate in radio call-in shows and "open phone" times. Whether the topic is food, health, beauty, or even sex, get on the phone with an animal issue tie-in!

*Number in parentheses indicates place where items with slogan can be purchased; see "Sources" at end of chapter.

- Arrange a series of talks and/or debates at a local community college, church, or civic center. To line up speakers, find out who in your community is most actively working with homeless animals, arranging demonstrations, and promoting vegetarianism. Once you have done your homework, and practiced in front of a mirror and friends, you may want to deliver your own talks.

- Make (or order) leaflets to distribute. Define your audience, and make sure your leaflet answers the questions what, where, when, why, and who. It must tell people specifically what they can do to help. Include a phone number as a point of contact. Keep it concise, factual, and *readable*.

- Ask local schools and universities to include an animal rights class in the curriculum. In Terre Haute, Indiana, activist Judith Barad got her university to add an animal rights class to the philosophy department curriculum, with herself as the instructor. The class considers issues such as criteria for personhood, speciesism, the nature of interests and rights, and the use of animals for food and in experiments.

- Leave an animal rights message on your answering machine. Messages activists have used include:

  • The meat and dairy industries kill 14 million animals a day.
  • A chicken-processing plant can waste 100 million gallons of water in a single day.
  • There are 55 acres of rain forest in a quarter-pound hamburger.
  • The water used to produce a quarter-pound hamburger is equal to the amount used by a family of four in one month.
  • Eating animals may be hazardous to your health.
  • The best thing you can do for the environment today is to quit eating animals. At the tone, let me know you've gone vegetarian and I'll call you back within the hour.
  • I can't come to the phone—I'm shopping for cruelty-free products. I would be happy to send you a list of companies that don't test on animals if you leave your name and address at the tone.
  • After leaving a message for John or Sue, please call your legislators to get their support for (a piece of local legislation).
  • Do you know where your companion animals are? Don't let them roam unsupervised—they may be stolen for animal research. And when you hang up, go give them a hug.

- Let an animal rights button speak for you. Lawyer and activist Gary Francione wore a button every day to the Supreme Court when he clerked for Justice Sandra Day O'Connor. Try: "Fur is Dead"(1), "Animals Are Not Ours to Eat, Wear, or Experiment On"(1), "Love Animals, Don't Eat Them"(2), "I'm Warm-Hearted: I Don't Wear Fur"(3), "Animal Research: Taxes for Torture"(4), "Rats Have Rights"(5), "Choose Cruelty-Free"(5), "*Against* Animal Testing"(6), "Meat-Free Zone"(7), and "I Don't Eat My Friends"(7). Or make your own, e.g., "Shameless Agitator" and "Boycott Gillette."

- Little cards can say a few dozen appropriate words, too. For that close encounter with the woman in dead minks on the elevator or the man in the beaver-collar flight jacket, there are graphic, pictorial cards that say, "Excuse me for approaching you, but we would like you to meet the previous owner of your fur coat," or "Here's what your furrier never told you"(1).

- Order **PETA**'s comprehensive manual, "The PETA Guide to Becoming an Activist" ($5 for nonmembers, $4.50 for members). It's a great "how to" for the novice (and even somewhat experienced) activist.

## SOURCES

1. **PETA,** P.O. Box 42516, Washington, DC 20015; (301) 770-7444.
2. **The Vegetarian Resource Group,** P.O. Box 1463, Baltimore, MD 21203; (301) 366-VEGE.
3. **Friends of Animals,** P.O. Box 120016, Stamford, CT 06912-0016, Department 228; 1-800-631-2212.
4. **Animal Rights Mobilization,** P.O. Box 1553, Williamsport, PA 17703; (717) 322-3252.
5. **British Union for the Abolition of Vivisection (BUAV),** 16a Crane Grove, London N7 8LB, England. Note: "Rats Have Rights" buttons are also available from **PETA.**
6. **The Body Shop,** 45 Horsehill Road, Cedar Knolls, NJ 07927-2003; 1-800-541-2535.
7. **Farm Animal Reform Movement (FARM),** Box 70123, Washington, DC 20088; (301) 530-1737.

# 5 JOIN A COALITION OF PROFESSIONALS

Responsibility is a great thing. To shoulder responsibility, not to shirk it. If we learned early in life not to avoid responsibility, the world would be brighter.

—ALBERT SCHWEITZER

## THE PROBLEM

All citizens have a right to be heard on moral issues, including matters that involve tax dollars, yet laypeople are often pompously dismissed by the professional organizations whose behaviors and opinions they are trying to change. "We'll police ourselves," say the psychologists. "No outside intervention," cry the veterinarians. Well, change *can* be effected internally; and animal rights activists *within* the professions are gathering together to make a difference in their own fields. For example, more than 20,000 physicians signed a petition condemning U.S. Surgical Corporation for using dogs when training salespeople to use its surgical staplers (over 1,000 dogs a year are killed after the stapling demonstrations); and nurses have united to change the age-old practice of teaching student RNs intubation by pushing a tube down kittens' throats instead of using a model such as Baby Air-In (by **Medical Plastics,** Gatesville, TX).

## THE SOLUTION

If you are a professional, join (or if you know a professional, encourage her/him to join) one of the following groups:

- **Physicians Committee for Responsible Medicine (PCRM),** P.O. Box 6322, Washington, DC 20015; (202) 686-2210.
An organization working to replace needless and cruel experiments on animals with an emphasis on preventive health care for humans and non-animal research methods. Their motto (and that of Hippocrates, the "father of modern medicine"): "First, do no harm."

- **Association of Veterinarians for Animal Rights (AVAR),** P.O. Box 6269, Vacaville, CA 95696; (707) 451-1391.
An organization working from the "premise that all animals have interests and intrinsic values that are independent of the interests and values of others" and under the assumption that veterinarians, by virtue of their training and career motivation, should be at the forefront of the advancement of animal rights.

- **National Association of Nurses Against Vivisection (NANAV),** P.O. Box 42210, Washington, DC 20015; (301) 770-8968.
NANAV "unites members of the nursing profession who are committed to the abolition of animal experimentation and the redistribution of precious health-care dollars."

- **Animal Legal Defense Fund (ALDF),** 1363 Lincoln Avenue, San Rafael, CA 94901; (415) 459-0885.
The ALDF is "a national group of about three hundred lawyers that litigates and lobbies for legislation to improve the treatment of animals."

- **Medical Research Modernization Committee (MRMC),** P.O. Box 6036, Grand Central Station, New York, NY 10163-6018; (212) 876-1368.
MRMC is "comprised of health-care professionals who lend their training, experience and expertise to evaluate the medical and/or scientific merit of research modalities in order to identify archaic methods and to promote sensible, reliable and efficient methods of research."

● **Psychologists for the Ethical Treatment of Animals (PsyETA),** P.O. Box 87, New Gloucester, ME 04260; (207) 926-4817.

PsyETA "works to *reduce* the number of animals used in each psychological study; to *replace* animals in research with cell cultures, statistical data, clinical cases, computers, and other alternatives; and to *refine* experimental design and methods to diminish use of animals and enhance the well-being of animals used."

# 6 TEAM UP

I get by with a little help from my friends.
                              —THE BEATLES

## THE PROBLEM

Working by yourself to change the world can be a lonely prospect; and the power of a group demonstrates that, in *addition* to the power of the individual, the whole is (frequently) greater than the sum of its parts. Becoming part of a team of concerned citizens, having a support system to lean on in times of frustration, pooling information and sharing ideas with others, or just pairing up, can make your life brighter and lighten your load.

## THE SOLUTION

- Link up with other people who share your concern for animals by advertising to find them: put notices on neighborhood bulletin boards, in health-food stores, laundromats, supermarkets, book-stores, and community newspapers. (For example, "Person interested in animal protection issues seeks others to form a group; call Pam at 123-4567." Or "Come join like-minded people who want to work for the animals and the Earth; call 123-4567.") Also, ask friendly radio announcers to put out a call for people who care about animals.

- Talk to other people with dogs in the park. Committed to seeing that their companion animals get plenty of fresh air and exercise, these folks are likely candidates for animal protection activism.
- Throw a regular letter-writing/sign-making work party. When animal legislation is pending, or animal issues are hot in your town, or the whole country is preparing to celebrate World Vegetarian Day, spend a few hours with other like-minded people doing work while enjoying vegan (fully vegetarian) snacks and/or an animal rights film. Check your library or contact **PETA** to borrow films free of charge.
- Advertise a monthly vegetarian pot-luck picnic or party. If attendance is slim at first, it always picks up as word-of-mouths-receiving-great-food spreads. Before the meal, provide guests with recipe cards and nutritional facts, and get people working together on a project, like brainstorming or planning a protest rally.
- Host a cruelty-free cosmetics party, the 1990s counterpart to Tupperware parties! Invite friends, co-workers, relatives and neighbors to sample perfumes and cosmetics from an **Aveda** representative, located at 321 Lincoln Street NE, Minneapolis, MN 55413; 1-800-328-0849, or from any of a number of cruelty-free companies you can contact with the help of **Beauty Without Cruelty,** 175 W. 12th Street, 12G, New York, NY 10011; (212) 989-8073. Now that Avon has stopped testing on animals, you may again opt for "Avon calling," but beware of animal ingredients.
- Get permission to place a permanent bulletin board (e.g., "ANIMAL WORLD") in a local store or at your post office. Provide space for lost-and-found animals or those who are looking for homes (photos are a plus), animal rights information, local news about animal happenings, and group newsletters.
- Start a "phone tree"—a calling system designed to reach a lot of people with very little effort on any one person's part. It works this way: when you need to reach a large number of people, you call three people who each call three others, who in turn each call three more people, and so on. Keep the tree updated and be sure to toss out "dead wood"—people who promise to make their calls but don't. Phone trees can help alert members to meetings and demonstrations, and mobilize activity on pressing issues (e.g., generate calls to an elected official to request s/he vote a particular way). Pig wrestling in Martin County, Florida, and beaver mis-

management at Reineman Sanctuary in New York were halted
largely because activists kept the phone lines humming.

- Join **PETA**'s national phone tree, (301) 770-7444. PETA will link
  you to activists in your area who can be called or can call you
  when quick action is needed on national, regional, or local animal
  issues.

- *Hook up with others on computer networks:*

  • **Amnet** is a nonprofit organization whose mission is "to promote
  the interests and well-being of animals and concern for the environment upon which they depend." Amnet contains three on-line
  computer services: "Animal Tracks" (contains submenus on animal rights issues in the form of messages and text files); "Litter
  Box" (contains submenus on special interest groups); and "Feed
  Back" (allows you to send private messages to the system operator
  only). For more information, contact: AMNET, P.O. Box 9517,
  Fort Collins, CO 80525; computer: (303) 223-1297; voice: (303)
  223-1154; netMail address: 104/65.

  • **The Institute for Global Communications (IGC),** a division
  of the nonprofit Tides Foundation, sponsors several international
  computer networks for the peace and ecology movements. These
  networks provide two basic services: electronic bulletin board systems ("conferences") and electronic mail. The IGC networks include PeaceNet and Econet and provide access to other networks,
  such as GreenNet in England. (When you join IGC you get access
  to all the networks.) The cost is very low, and in most parts of
  the U.S. you can access the network via a local call to TeleNet,
  a common carrier, so there are no long-distance charges. The ICG
  networks are compatible with virtually any personal computer or
  computer terminal outfitted with a modem; you do not need to be
  computer literate to use the system! The animal rights conference
  (part of EcoNet) is called "gn.animals" and covers "news, information, policy discussions and action alerts on all aspects of
  animal rights, both domestic and agricultural." For more information, contact: Institute for Global Communications, 3228 Sacramento Street, San Francisco, CA 94115; (415) 923-0900.

  • **"Usenet"** (a major network) has a "Newsgroups" discussion
  forum devoted to vegetarian issues—"Rec.Food.Veg."—which

also sometimes generates animal rights discussions. There is a fee for a local-access number.

• Speak with your favorite computer buff, contact your community computer club, or visit a PC store for more information on how to access these systems.

# 7 | EDUCATE TO LIBERATE

No army can withstand the strength of an idea whose time has come.
—Victor Hugo

How many a man has dated a new era in his life from reading a book!
—Henry David Thoreau

## THE PROBLEM

When your neighbor asks, "What's wrong with bullfighting?" "How do you get your protein?" "Is it true greyhounds from the track go to research?" "Do sled dogs enjoy racing?" "Is tobacco tested on animals?" or "Is the leghold trap illegal in Florida?" do you know the answers?

## THE SOLUTION

Empowerment through learning. Here's our recommended reading list (the ones with an asterisk are available from PETA):

### Must-Read

- *Animal Liberation,** by Peter Singer (New York: New York Review, 1990). A basic primer on animal rights.

- *Diet for a New America,** by John Robbins (Walpole, N.H.: Still-point Publishing, 1987). A moving and well-documented book that describes the inhumane and unhealthy conditions under which animals are raised for food and how our health and ecological well-being are linked to the adoption of a vegan diet.
- *In Defense of Animals,** edited by Peter Singer (New York: Harper & Row, 1985). Excellent essays on factory farming, zoos, and other animal rights issues. Includes a chapter by PETA chairperson Alex Pacheco, who recounts his experiences while working in the laboratory where he discovered the famous Silver Spring monkeys.

## General Animal Rights

- *The Case for Animal Rights,* by Dr. Tom Regan (Berkeley, Calif.: University of California Press, 1983). A philosophical analysis of animal rights.
- *Fettered Kingdoms,* by John Bryant (Washington, D.C.: PETA, 1982). A short, moving description of our relationship to other-than-human beings, based on the premise that other-than-humans are often kept as slaves, toys, and cheap burglar alarms.
- *Animals' Rights—Considered in Relation to Social Progress,* by Henry Salt (Clarks Summit, Penn.: International Society for Animal Rights, 1980). First published in 1892, Salt's book explores our attitudes toward animals with insight and compassion.
- *Animal Rights and Human Obligations,* by Peter Singer and Tom Regan (Englewood Cliffs, N.J.: Prentice-Hall, 1976). A collection of writings exploring our relations with other-than-human beings, by thinkers such as Aristotle, Charles Darwin, and Tom Regan.
- *Inhumane Society: The American Way of Exploiting Animals,* by Michael Fox (New York: St. Martin's Press, 1990). Describes how the magnitude of animal suffering caused by humankind is more insidious and pervasive than that caused by any natural scourges. A compelling indictment of the veterinary community and other animal industries, and a convincing case for the rights of animals.
- *On the Fifth Day: Animal Rights and Human Ethics,* edited by Richard Knowles Morris and Michael W. Fox (Washington, D.C.: Acropolis, 1978). An anthology of essays by prominent philosophers, ecologists, biologists, lawyers, animal behaviorists, and

theologians, who address the complex question of humanity's relation to other-than-human beings.

## Vivisection/Animal Experimentation

- *The Cruel Deception,* by Robert Sharpe (England: Thorson's Publishing Group, 1988); distributed by the **American Anti-Vivisection Society,** Suite 204 Noble Plaza, 801 Old York Road, Jenkintown, PA 19046. Shows how animal experiments consistently fail to improve human health and even add to the burden of disease.
- *Slaughter of the Innocent,* by Hans Ruesch (New York: Civitas, Swain, 1983). A description of the vivisection industry with graphic examples of the human health hazards of animal tests and animal-based pharmacology.
- *Alternatives to Current Uses of Animals in Research, Testing and Education,* Martin Stephens (Washington, D.C.: Humane Society of the United States, 1986).

## Vegetarianism/Veganism/Factory Farming

- *A Vegetarian Sourcebook,* by Keith Akers (New York: Putnam, 1983; and Arlington, Va.: Vegetarian Press, 1983). Contains all the arguments and facts about the nutritional, ecological, and ethical basis of this humane diet.
- *Animal Factories,\** by Jim Mason and Peter Singer (New York: Crown, 1985). An exposé of modern "factory farming" and its detrimental effects on the animals and the small farmer.
- *The McDougall Plan,* by John and Mary McDougall (Piscataway, N.J.: New Century Publishers, 1983); located at 220 Old New Brunswick Road, Piscataway, NJ 08854. A physician who specializes in diet-related diseases, Dr. McDougall's plan encourages a life-style that best supports our natural tendencies to heal and stay healthy. A well-researched guidebook to veganism, including recipes.

- *The Power of The Plate,* by Neal Barnard, M.D. (Summertown, Tenn.: Book Publishing Co., 1990). A precise and ground-breaking guide to what a vegan diet can do for you. Drawing on the latest research and the thoughts and ideas of leading experts, Dr. Barnard makes a convincing case for rebuilding your menu.
- *Judy Brown's Guide to Natural Foods Cooking,** by Judy Brown (Summertown, Tenn.: The Book Publishing Co., 1989). Over 200 recipes featuring whole grains, legumes, vegetables, fruits, and soy foods, plus many vegan macrobiotic dishes.
- *The New Farm Vegetarian Cookbook,** by Louise Hagler (Summertown, N.J.: The Book Publishing Co., 1988). Over 200 recipes using soyfoods, traditional legumes and more. Everything is cholesterol- and lactose-free. Recipes are low in fat and sodium and easy to prepare.

## Fiction

- *The Plague Dogs,* by Richard Adams (New York: Alfred A. Knopf, 1978). Two dogs escape from a laboratory where they have been horribly tortured. Also a video (ask at video stores).
- *Doctor Rat,* by William Kotzwinkle (New York: Avon, 1971). A witty but gruesome tale of animals in one laboratory.

## Religion

- *The Moral Status of Animals,* by Steven R. L. Clark (Oxford, England: Oxford University Press, 1977).
- *Food For the Spirit: Vegetarianism and the World Religions,** by Steven Rosen (New York: Bala Books, 1987); located at 268 West 23rd Street, New York, NY 10011.
- *Judaism and Vegetarianism,* by Richard Schwartz (Marblehead, Mass.: Micah, 1988).
- *Christianity and the Rights of Animals,* by Andrew Linzey (New York: Crossroad, 1987).

## Companion Animals

- *Mother Knows Best,* by Carol Lea Benjamin (New York: Howell, 1985). Dog training designed to mimic that of canine mothers, using body language and games and spoken words, and emphasizing dogs' natural behavior.
- *Vegetarian Cats & Dogs,* by James Peden (Hayden Lake, Idaho: Harbingers of a New Age, 1990); located at 12100 Brighton Street, Hayden Lake, ID 83835 (price $12.95). A sourcebook for introducing your companion animals to a vegetarian or vegan diet.
- *Dr. Pitcairn's Complete Guide to Natural Health,* by Dr. Richard and Susan Pitcairn (Emaus, Penn.: Rodale Press: 1982). Sets the standard for companion animal natural health-care.
- *The PETA Companion Animal Record Book\** (Washington, D.C.: PETA, 1988). Helps you keep track of your friend's health, history, likes and dislikes, personality and special needs. Includes checklists as well as basic tips on regular health care and emergencies, choosing a veterinarian, and traveling.

## Miscellaneous

**Fur**
- *North American Fur Sources and Trade in the Eighties,* by Merritt Clifton (Washington, D.C.: Humane Society of the United States, 1988).

**Wool**
- *Pulling the Wool,* by Christine Townend (Sydney, Australia: Hale and Iremonger, 1985).

**Zoos**
- *Beyond the Bars,* by Virginia McKenna (Wellingborough, Northamptonshire: Thorsons, 1987).

**Feminism**
- *The Sexual Politics of Meat,* by Carol Adams (New York: Continuum, 1990).

**Hunting**
- *Man Kind? Our Incredible War on Wildlife,* by Cleveland Amory (New York: Dell, 1974); available for $4.95 prepaid from **Fund for Animals,** 200 W. 57th Street, New York, NY 10019; (212) 246-2096.
- *The American Hunting Myth,* by Ron Baker (New York: Vantage Press, 1985); available for $12.55 (members) or $13.95 (nonmembers) plus postage from **PETA.**

**Racism:** • *The Dreaded Comparison* by Marjourie Spiegel (New York: Mirror Books, 1990).

**Activism** • *PETA's Guide to Animal Rights Organizing,* **PETA.**

**Cosmetics** • *Animal Testing and Consumer Products,* by Heidi J. Welsh (Washington, D.C.: Investor Responsibility Research Center, 1990).

**Maternity** • *Pregnancy, Children, and the Vegan Diet,* Michael Klaper, M.D. (Umatilla, Fla.: Gentle World, 1987); available for $8.95 + $1.50 shipping and handling from **EarthSave,** 706 Frederick Street, Santa Cruz, CA 95062.

**Children** • *Black Beauty, Charlotte's Web, The Hundred and One Dalmatians, The Story of Ferdinand, Blueberries for Sal* (available from many publishers and libraries).

• *I Love Animals and Broccoli Activity Book* (for reading-age children) and *I Love Animals and Broccoli Coloring Book,* available from **The Vegetarian Resource Group,** P.O. Box 1463, Baltimore, MD 21203; (301) 366-VEGE.

## Magazines

• *Vegetarian Times,* P.O. Box 570, Oak Park, IL 60303; (708) 848-8100; 12 issues, $24.95/year.

• *The Animals' Voice Magazine,* P.O. Box 16955, No. Hollywood, CA 91615; 1-800-82-VOICE; 6 issues, $18/year.

• *PETA News,* P.O. Box 42516, Washington, DC 20015; (301) 770-7444; 6 issues, as well as 2 issues of PETA Kids, Action Alerts, and other mailings; $15/year (membership fee).

**Note: PETA** has fact sheets on dozens of topics. Write to request one for a particular subject or for a full list of topics—or order a complete set (*Facts for Activists,* $7).

# 8 | ACTIVISM ON THE JOB

The fate of animals is of greater importance to me than the fear of appearing ridiculous; it is indissolubly connected with the fate of men.

— EMILE ZOLA

## THE PROBLEM

For most of us, roughly 2,000–3,000 hours annually (80,000–120,000 hours in a professional lifetime!) are spent at work—that's equal to 9 to 14 uninterrupted years of our lives. It's comforting to know that, at the office and "in the field," there are hundreds of ways to help the animals.

## THE SOLUTION

Singers sing about animals, writers write about animals, and teachers teach about animals. No matter what you do, you can be an activist. The Serios family donates fruits, vegetables, and nuts from their family produce store to a sanctuary for rescued animals. Marvin Kraushar, M.D., an ophthalmologist, took time from his practice to give expert testimony in favor of a ban on eye-irritancy tests traditionally performed on rabbits. Ken Edpemon, a carpenter, built a beautiful booth for the local animal protection group. Gloria's Trucking Company in Boston distributes animal rights magazines free with every drop-off.

- See if your employer has a "matching funds program" through which your company doubles employees' donations to favorite charities.

- If you have a staff cafeteria or dining room, ask the management to feature vegetarian options and to get rid of veal. Give the head of the food service and/or the chef some recipe suggestions or the *Executive Plan* by the Physicians Committee for Responsible Medicine (PCRM), which contains institution-size, cholesterol-free recipes, posters, nutrition briefs, and card messages for diners to enjoy and learn from. Get the support of other employees to show that healthful meals are in demand and would be appreciated. Contact **PCRM** at P.O. Box 6322, Washington, DC 20015; (202) 686-2210.

- Ask the orders manager to talk to suppliers about replacing office products such as Gillette (Papermate) pens and (Wite-Out) correction fluid, as well as those from other companies that, as of this writing, still test on animals, with cruelty-free office products, such as Quill pens and Rotex Correctsafe correction fluid. Contact **Quill** at P.O. Box 4700, Lincolnshire, IL 60197-4700, (708) 634-4800; or P.O. Box 50-050, Ontario, CA 91761-1050, (714) 988-3200. Contact **Rotex** at International Rotex, Inc., P.O. Box 20697, Reno, NV 89515; (702) 356-8356. Make sure bathroom soaps are from companies on the cruelty-free list too (see chapter 1, "The Ugly Side of Beauty") and are labeled as such to show visitors and staff.

- When you've finished reading your animal protection magazines and literature, bring them to work for others to peruse: set up a rack in common areas such as lounges, dining rooms, and bathrooms.

- Wear a button to work. Let colleagues know how you feel about cruelty-free living and other animal issues.

- If your office has a speaker series, invite an animal protection professional to show a film, give a talk, or lead or be part of a seminar or panel discussion.

- Display an animal rights poster near your desk or work station as a conversation starter and thought provoker.

- Host a vegetarian breakfast in your workplace, introducing co-workers to eco-sensible fare in a friendly, nonthreatening way.

- Get on food and organizing committees to ensure that all staff parties and picnics have vegetarian/vegan options and that staff incentives don't include fur or other offensive prizes. Help choose convention sites and hotels to ensure that healthful vegetarian food will be served.
- Mail carriers can distribute free fact sheets and pamphlets on their routes.
- If you work in or for a shopping mall, building company, car dealership, or school, make sure the establishment or institution has a policy never to permit animal acts or exhibits, to use harmless alternatives to gluetraps, never to institute a pigeon poisoning program or use harmful lawn chemicals, and to use an electronic security system rather than guard dogs (who are usually grossly mistreated and deprived ex-companion animals).

# 9 | SAFEGUARD YOUR ANIMAL FRIEND

Not to hurt our humble brethren is our first duty to them, but to stop there is not enough. We have a higher mission—to be of service to them wherever they require it.

—FRANCIS OF ASSISI, 1181–1220,
quoted in the *Life* by Saint Bonaventura.

## THE PROBLEM

Companion animals are vulnerable to theft and human mischief. For example, *bunchers* are scurrilous beings who make their living cruising neighborhoods for dogs and cats whom they sell to dealers, guard dog companies, and unscrupulous breeders. In South Dakota, a fur trader was caught using cat skins; satanic cults in Florida have cleaned whole blocks of cats; and "expensive" dogs have been known to end up in other people's living rooms. In 1984, the prestigious Mayo Clinic in Minnesota was found to be harboring seven of thirteen dogs who had been stolen from farm homes in Mower County.

## Did You Know?

- According to Census figures, 1 of every 5 people in the United States "owns" a dog. Every year, approximately 10 percent of U.S. companion dogs are reported missing. Mary Warner, founder and director of Action 81 (a group dedicated to public awareness of companion animal theft), believes that about half of those—or 1 in 20 of all companion dogs—may be stolen.

- In Illinois in 1987, 228,000 dogs were reported missing.
- Close to 12 million dogs and cats end up in pounds each year. Of these, fewer than 15 percent return to their original homes (a low of 4 percent in New York, a high of 15 percent in Palm Beach, Florida), and fewer than 15 percent of impounded dogs and cats are otherwise re-homed. The majority (over 8 million) are destroyed or, from some facilities, sold as guard dogs or for experiments.
- It is *conservatively* estimated that 2 million dogs are stolen each year.
- Nationwide, thefts peak in the summer.
- Laboratories and medical schools nationwide use more than 300,000 dogs and 100,000 cats each year.
- Stolen animals in the United States are sold to researchers, held for ransom, used for shark bait or to train pitbull dogs, used as fur trim, eaten, and tortured in cult rituals.

## THE SOLUTION

Take measures to safeguard your companion animals. Here's how:

- *Be vigilant*. Never leave dogs unsupervised in a yard or chained or tied up alone. Cats should be allowed out only with you and are better off indoors if the alternative is to have them disappear. Animals left unattended in cars are a favorite target for thieves.
- *Photograph*. Always have current photographs of your companion animals in case they turn up missing.
- *Tag and Tattoo*. A good identification system includes both a tag and a tattoo.

  • An ID tag should be attached to a collar made out of ⅜″ elastic (which won't strangle the animal if caught on a hook or tree limb) for cats and young puppies with your name, address, and phone number in indelible ink. Have several in reserve and replace promptly if damaged. For adult dogs, a standard nylon (*not* leather) collar should suffice. Check for sizing by fitting two fingers comfortably between the collar and the neck.

• Use a painless, permanent tattoo (tags can be lost or removed, rendering the animal conveniently anonymous). Veterinarians, shelters, pounds, and laboratories often check for tattoos, and many animals have been happily reunited with their families because they were "wearing" tattooed identification on their skin (on thigh or belly, as ears can be cut off).

• *Organizations that can help:*

**National Dog Registry,** located at Box 116, Woodstock, NY 12498-0116; (914) 679-BELL, has tattooed and registered more than 2.4 million dogs—identified by the guardian's social security number. NDR charges a one-time fee of $35, which covers all animals in a household. NDR has agents throughout the country and claims a 97 percent recovery rate. To report a lost dog with a social security number tattoo, call 1-800-NDR-DOGS.

**Tattoo-A-Pet,** located at 1625 Emmons Ave., Suite 1H, Brooklyn, NY, 11235; 1-800-828-8667, has approximately 1 million dogs registered—coded by state, agent doing the tattoo, and a number for each animal—and two thousand authorized facilities nationwide. Claiming a 99 percent recovery rate, TAP has two thousand agents around the U.S. The fee is $10, plus $10 for the tattoo.

**Action 81,** located at Route 3, Box 6000, Berryville, VA 22611; (703) 955-1278, is a dog theft awareness group. Contact them if you have information on animal theft rings.

**Your local humane society, animal shelter or animal rights group** may be able to provide you with a list of dealers and research laboratories in your area. By federal law, these facilities must allow police officers access to search for a missing animal.

● *In case your friend turns up missing.* Scour the neighborhood, check the Lost and Found section of your newspapers, post clear signs, visit shelters daily, and question mail carriers, children, and neighbors for information. *Don't give up.*

• Call out at night when it's quiet and look under houses, down drainage ditches, up in trees, and in abandoned houses.

• Spray-paint big, simple messages on scrap plywood (look down alleys for discarded lumber) and place them at intersections so that drivers can't miss them. Keep it simple, e.g., "BLACK DOG LOST, CALL 123-4567." Offering a reward often helps. Make sure someone is home to take phone calls; or if you have an answering machine, make sure callers know that you are the one looking for the "BLACK DOG."

• Contact all local veterinarians, shelters and pounds, laboratories and dealers, and leave cards on bulletin boards. No matter what pounds and shelters tell you over the telephone, go there *personally* no less than once a day and be sure to show the workers photos of the lost animal. Also check with sanitation crews who remove dead animals from roads.

• If you have recently moved, leave notices with neighbors in the old area and check with animal agencies there (or send a reliable friend or relative who *knows* the missing animal to look for her/him).

• Put an ad in the "lost-and-found" section of local and community papers, and distribute fliers door-to-door.

• Keep looking! Missing animals have been reunited with persistent humans after many months of searching.

# 10 FROM TOFU PUP TO... GARBANZO CAT?

The U.S. Department of Agriculture uses the term "4-D" to indicate flesh that's considered unfit for human consumption. The "D's" are: dead, dying, disabled, and diseased. In all but a few states, flesh from 4-D animals can be sold to pet food manufacturers. . . . [Jim] Mason and [Peter] Singer report an average of 15 million pounds of cancerous tissues a year [added to slaughterhouse reject piles—much of which is rendered into] "by-products" on pet food labels.

—BARBARA LYNN PEDEN,
*Dogs and Cats Go Vegetarian*

## THE PROBLEM

Each year, we buy 100 million cats and dogs in America $5 billion worth of food; these commercial "pet foods" (full of organ meats, veins, and the skin between pigs' ears and chickens' toes) contribute to the suffering of both companion and farm animals. Many vegetarians recognize that many "pet food" ingredients come from the very same slaughterhouses that violently produce flesh intended for human consumption, and that commercial "pet foods" generally consist of the waste products of the slaughter industry, including diseased, cancerous flesh marked "unfit for human consumption," as well as the same chemical residues passed on in flesh slated for human (in)digestion. In the U.S. cancer is the major cause of nonaccidental death in cats and dogs and the second greatest in humans.

In the wild, dogs are omnivorous and cats carnivorous, so many people hesitate to provide these now domesticated species with a vegetarian or vegan diet. Sure, nobody can argue that it is "natural" for dogs and cats to live on a pure vegetarian diet, but neither can they argue that it is "natural" for these animals to be eating preslaughtered cows and pigs, or even living in our homes. Thanks to the research and work of Barbara Lynn Peden and others, we now know that dogs and cats can do very well on a nutritionally sound vegetarian, or even vegan, diet.

## THE SOLUTION

● For both dogs and cats, we recommend Vegepet supplements, which come in three forms: Vegedog, Vegekit, and Vegecat, available from **Harbingers of a New Age,** 12100 Brighton Street, Hayden Lake, ID 83814; (208) 772-7753. Add Vegepet supplements to various vegetable-, legume-, and grain-based recipes. Two sample recipes:

### GARBANZO CAT CHOW (Peden)

⅜ cup sprouted or cooked garbanzo beans
1½ tbsp. nutritional yeast powder
1 tbsp. chopped or grated vegetable(s)
1 tbsp. oil
½ tsp. Vegecat
⅓ tsp. soy sauce

### VEGAN DOG BISCUIT (PETA recipe collection)

9 cups whole wheat flour
1 cup nutritional yeast
1 tbsp. salt
1 tbsp. garlic powder
1 tbsp. Vegedog (for optimal nutrition)

Mix dry ingredients. Add approximately 3 cups water. Knead into a pliable dough. Roll out until ⅛″ thick. Cut into shapes. Bake for 10–15 minutes at 350 degrees F. After turning off oven, leave biscuits in overnight or equivalent so they become hard and crunchy.

- Cats are more likely to need extra incentives to eat unfamiliar foods than are dogs. Peden provides the following "helpful hints": use textured soy protein with simulated flesh flavor (e.g., "ham" bits and "beef mince," available from some health food and Seventh Day Adventist stores); serve the food warm; sprinkle nutritional yeast on top; temporarily add soy milk, avocado, or a little more oil; and mix in a favorite seasoning such as tomato sauce or soup.

- If the new diet meets resistance, you can try mixing the old and new foods together, gradually increasing the proportion of vegetarian food.

- Many dogs love spaghetti and other pastas, rice, and whole-grain bread combined with soups and sauces. In addition, there are prepared vegetarian dog foods, canned and kibble, including Nature's Recipe, available at **Wow-Bow Distributors,** 309 Burr Road, East Northport, NY 11731; (516) 499-8572.

- Cats' special  ary needs are more critical than dogs'; for example, they can suffer loss of eyesight and die if they are deprived of taurine, which until recently was virtually impossible to find in a non-animal form (now available as a derivative of an organic, renewable, non-animal source). While most cats appear to do well on a vegetarian diet, some have not adapted so well. Monitor your companion *closely* when you switch her/him to a non-meat diet. (Harbingers of a New Age can answer any questions you might have.)

- Buy or borrow *Vegetarian Cats & Dogs,* by James Peden (Hayden Lake, Idaho: Harbingers of a New Age, 1990), price $12.95, to help you understand dogs' and cats' nutritional needs and identify and locate non-animal sources of essential components of cats' and dogs' diets like vitamin A, taurine, and arachidonic acid.

# 11 MAKING VACATION ARRANGEMENTS FOR ANIMALS

I wish people would realize that animals are totally dependent on us, helpless, like children, a trust that is put upon us . . .
> —**JAMES HERRIOT,** from a television interview, 1978

The fidelity of a dog is a precious gift demanding no less binding moral responsibilities than the friendship of a human being.
> —**KONRAD LORENZ,** *Man Meets Dog*

## THE PROBLEM

Holiday travel plans that include taking your companion animals with you, or trying to figure out comfortable, appropriate arrangements for them if they must stay behind, can be difficult and stressful. Here are a number of options designed to make it easier to make informed decisions.

## THE SOLUTION

### Going with You

- *On the road.* Don't feed cats or dogs within an hour of departure, and carry water for rest stops. Install shade blinds on windows, and *never* leave dogs and cats unattended in parked cars or out of your eyesight, especially in summer. Most **Holiday Inns** allow cats and dogs of any size in the rooms (call 1-800-HOLIDAY for information on inns at or near your destination). "Touring with Towser," a directory of U.S. hotels and motels that accommodate other-than-human guests, is available from **Professional Services,** P.O. Box 877, Young America, MN 55399; $1.50 prepaid.

• When traveling by car with a cat, confine her/him in a sturdy, well-ventilated carrier big enough for her/him to stand up and turn around in comfortably. Line it with a towel and a tiny litter tray. The carriers should have a door that lets you see in and lets your friend see both you and the inside of the car, but blocks out views of oncoming cars and flashing lights, which can be frightening. If possible, secure the carrier to the seat with a belt. Open the carrier several days before the trip and let the cat get used to it (try a little catnip). **Note:** a cardboard box with holes punched into it is dangerous because cats can often squeeze out, and the box provides almost no protection in an accident.
• Dogs can either be put in sturdy travel kennels or ride unrestrained. Stay alert to prevent possible escapes. Some stores and catalogs sell companion animal restraint devices that are similar to, or can be used with, seatbelts. A Pet Safety Belt is available for $19.95 from **Pedigrees,** (716) 352-1232. Stop to walk dogs often!

• *Flying.* Choose a direct, nonstop flight. Avoid heavy traffic days, such as holidays and weekends. Reserve space for your companion well in advance, as airlines limit the number of other-than-human spaces per flight. Don't feed your companion animal solid food for at least six hours before flight time, but a little water and a peppy "walk" are a must before boarding. The kennel your companion travels in must be USDA approved (most airlines and pet stores sell them).

• If your animal friend is small (can fit into a carry-on kennel that goes under your seat), choose an airline that allows him/her to fly in the passenger compartment with you. This is far less frightening to animals and much safer than riding in the cargo space.
• If your animal friend *must* fly cargo, use only a direct, nonstop flight, making sure to fly at night in summer, during the day in

winter, and never during temperature extremes (animals can freeze to death, suffocate, or die of heat prostration in cargo holds—especially if there is a delay). Be sure you or someone very reliable sees the animal safely aboard, meets the arriving flight, and knows how to raise cain if the animal doesn't arrive on time. Sturdy, roomy, well-ventilated carriers and clear identification are essential (accustom the animal to the kennel at home long before the departure date). Recommended carriers can be purchased from most airlines. For a travel pamphlet with further tips, send a self-addressed, stamped envelope to **Washington Humane Society,** 7319 Georgia Avenue NW, Washington, DC 20012; or call (202) 333-4010.

## Staying Behind

- Your animal companions love you and will miss you, so greet and leave them with this foremost in your mind. Always remember to say goodbye. Use a kind, "stay," look directed into your friend's eyes and say, very reassuringly and firmly, "I'll be back." When you return, always say, *first* thing, "I'm back." The idea that your absence will not be forever is reinforced in this simple way.

- Keep your dogs or cats safely at home, rather than board them out with strangers. There's a lot to be said for familiar surroundings, i.e., they are generally the safest and least stressful. Try to find a responsible (adult) friend or relative to stay at your home or to come by *at least* three times a day to keep an eye on the animals and tend to their needs (i.e., allow them to relieve themselves). Even if there are ample provisions, accidents happen and someone should make safety checks often. If you can't find someone you know and trust, explore a "pet-sitting" service that has *several* verifiable and reliable references—from a humane society, veterinarians, and bona fide clients.

- Make sure the chosen caretaker has all the important information posted near the telephone, including emergency numbers (veterinary night service and numbers where you can be reached).

- If you *must* board: Veterinary hospitals are not recommended because animals can be exposed to illnesses and can often sense the pain of others around them. Be very careful when choosing a boarding facility—smiling people can run little shops of horrors. Humane officers have frightening stories to tell, such as animals stacked in crates during peak boarding seasons, and families returning home to find that their friends had "escaped." Ask friends for references, and check with your local Chamber of Commerce and Department of Consumer Affairs for possible complaints against the facility. Make sure that you inspect the *entire* premises. If you are told that this is inconvenient or that insurance regulations prevent your inspection, head out the front door, pronto.

# 12 OBJECTING TO DISSECTING

What are we doing when we brainwash children in schools to cut open their fellow animals? Are we dangerously desensitizing them? Some of the most warped and blunted people I know are those who have gone through prolonged trainings of this sort.

> —**RICHARD D. RYDER,** from the Proceedings of the Symposium held by the Humane Education Council
> at Sussex University, 1980

If [man] is not to stifle human feelings, he must practice kindness toward animals, for he who is cruel to animals becomes hard also in his dealings with men. We can judge the heart of man by his treatment of animals.

> —**IMMANUEL KANT,** *Lectures on Ethics*

I . . . know that it was a waste of time for me to take about twenty-three years to be able to recognize a toad as an important entity and not merely an adjunct to other life, including my own.

> —**M. F. K. FISCHER,** *A Cordiall Water*

## THE PROBLEM

Every year between 3 and 6 million frogs—as well as many mice, chipmunks, sparrows, snakes, rats, rabbits, sharks, pigs, cats, dogs, and other animals—are dissected in U.S. schools. Nowadays, students and teachers are rethinking the value of this exercise. After all, how many people grow up to use their personal recollection of where exactly that frog's or cat's heart was and how long it took them to stop it from beating?

Although some students like Jenifer Graham of California and Maggie McCool of New Jersey have had to sue their schools for the right *not* to dissect or even watch dissection, with so many positive educational alternatives to dissection available, most students can make the case without a fight. For example:

- California law now gives students (grades K–12) the right to refuse to dissect, harm, or kill animals—as well as the right to substitute an alternative project, provided the instructor agrees that an acceptable alternative exists.
- A new faculty policy at the University of Colorado states that most undergraduates will "dissect" computer simulations rather than actual beings, while courses requiring other-than-human dissection will be so identified. At nearby Arapahoe Community College, students may opt out of dissecting but still must attend dissection labs.

## THE SOLUTION

The National Association of Biology Teachers recommends using humane alternatives to dissection, including computer displays (that allow the "frog" to be put back together again and hop from the screen!), films, videos, and plastic models. By heeding the following guidelines, you can end cruelty in the classroom. (If you have children in school, you can help them refuse to participate in lessons in insensitivity.)

- If you are a student, refuse to dissect. Put your feelings in writing to your teacher and principal, and try to involve your parents if you can. Parents, support your child's right to nonviolent education. **The Dissection Hotline,** 1-800-922-FROG (3764), exists *specifically* to help you protest animal dissection in the classroom; the **Animal Legal Defense Fund,** located at 1363 Lincoln Avenue, San Rafael, CA 94901, (415) 459-0885, sponsors the hotline and provides legal support for students who object to dissection. Don't be afraid to ask for help.
- Offer to complete an alternative project. Organizations such as AWI, PCRM, NEAVS, NAAHE, and SACA can help students,

teachers, and parents obtain appropriate classroom ideas and materials (see "Additional Resources" section below).

- Get other students to join you; form an animal rights group at school.
- Distribute leaflets about dissection to fellow students.
- Write letters to your school newspaper. Ask the reporters to do an article on dissection.
- If you aren't getting a positive response from your school, you may want to picket against dissection. Call the local television stations and newspapers in advance to let them know of your protest.
- Remember: animals delivered dead to classrooms did not die of natural causes: they were killed, usually by the crudest and cheapest methods, only because someone could make money selling their bodies. By cutting off the demand, cutting up animals will end.

## ADDITIONAL RESOURCES

- **Animal Welfare Institute (AWI),** P.O. Box 3650, Washington, DC 20007; (202) 337-2333. For grade-school- to high-school-level project ideas, write for their excellent book *The Endangered Species Handbook* (free to students).

- **Physicians Committee for Responsible Medicine (PCRM),** P.O. Box 6322, Washington, DC 20015; (202) 686-2210. They also publish *Alternatives in Medical Education* (free) and provide support for medical and veterinary medical students opposed to animal laboratories.

- **New England Anti-Vivisection Society (NEAVS),** 333 Washington Street, Suite 850, Boston, MA 02108; The Biology Methods Review Project (617) 523-2237. They provide a comprehensive thirty-one-page book of alternatives, *Alternatives in Biology Education: Non-Animal Methods,* edited by Alice Daniel. Free and available in bulk, *Alternatives* lists sources of computer programs, models, and films for elementary and high schools.

- **National Association for Humane and Environmental Education (NAHEE),** P.O. Box 362, East Haddam, CT 06432; (203)

434-8666. Provides educational materials for classrooms (primarily grades seven-twelve). Send $5 for NAHEE's Dissection Packet (includes specific alternatives to some of the most common animal-related biology experiments and dissections).

- **Student Action Corps for Animals (SACA),** P.O. Box 15588, Washington, DC 20003; Action Line (202) 543-8983. Provides over-the-phone counseling; in-depth dissection packet; book on non-animal alternatives ($2 or whatever you can afford); and information on organizing in high schools and working in local communities. For $7 membership, students receive newsletter, action alerts, and other mailings.

- **Humane Education Committee,** P.O. Box 445, Gracie Station, New York, NY 10028; (212) 410-3095. Serves as a consultant to teachers and activists on writing policy statements and on working with local Boards of Education.

# 13 GREAT-GRANDMA KNEW BEST

Purge me with hyssop, and I shall be clean: wash me, and I shall be whiter than snow.

**—Psalm 51:7**

## THE PROBLEM

Household products sold in stores can involve a variety of hidden hazards, ranging from potentially and known dangerous ingredients to environmentally destructive packaging. Commercially prepared cleaners, for example, may contain chemicals that can cause cancer, respiratory problems, or other illnesses in humans and companion animals.

Many commercial detergents also contain phosphates that end up in animals' river and stream homes. Even small amounts of them can cause huge increases in the growth of algae. When the algae die, microorganisms use up the water's oxygen, leaving untold numbers of fishes, crustaceans, and other aquatic animals to suffocate.

## THE "SOLUTION"

Dozens of safe and effective home recipes can be concocted from substances as inexpensive as baking soda and vinegar. Here are some suggestions:

## Cleansers

*Cooking utensils:* Let pots and pans soak in baking soda solution before washing.

*Copper cleaner:* Use a paste of lemon juice, salt, and flour; or rub vinegar and salt into the copper.

*Furniture polish:* Mix three-parts olive oil and one-part vinegar, or one-part lemon juice and two-parts vegetable oil. Use a soft cloth.

*General cleaner:* Mix baking soda with a small amount of water.

*Glass cleaner:* White vinegar or rubbing alcohol and water.

*Household cleaner:* Three tablespoons of baking soda mixed into one quart of warm water.

*Linoleum floor cleaner:* One cup of white vinegar mixed with two gallons of water to wash, club soda to polish.

*Mildew remover:* Lemon juice or white vinegar and salt.

*Stain remover, toilet bowl cleaner:* Vinegar.

*Wine/coffee stains:* Blot the fresh spill with a cloth soaked with club soda.

## Insect Repellents

*Ant control:* Pour a line of cream of tartar at the place where ants enter the house—they will not cross it.

*Ant repellent:* Wash countertops, cabinets, and floors with equal parts vinegar and water.

*Cockroach repellent:* Place whole bay leaves in several locations around kitchen.

*Flea and tick repellent:* Feed brewer's yeast and garlic tablets to companion animals. Place herbs such as fennel, rue, pennyroyal, and rosemary and/or eucalyptus seeds and leaves where the animal sleeps or on the animal to repel fleas.

*Mosquito repellent:* Eat brewer's yeast or take it in tablet form daily during the summer months.

*Mothballs:* Place cedar chips around clothes; dried lavender can be made into sachets and placed in drawers and closets.

## Miscellaneous

*Air freshener:* Leave an opened box of baking soda in the room, or add cloves and cinnamon to boiling water and simmer. Scent the house with fresh flowers or herbs; or open windows (in the winter, for about 15 minutes every morning).

*Drain opener:* Prevent clogging by using a drain stainer or by flushing the drain weekly with about a gallon of boiling water. If clogged, pour one-half-cup baking soda, then one-half-cup vinegar down the drain and cover it tightly for about a minute.

*Odor remover (spills and accidents):* On carpet or furniture, blot the fresh stain with a cloth soaked with cider vinegar.

*Water softener:* One-quarter cup vinegar in the final rinse.

## Resources

- For a more extensive list, write to **PETA** for a free pamphlet, titled "Homemade Household Product Recipes."

# 14 CREATE A BACKYARD SANCTUARY

I'm sure I've been a toad, one time or another. With bats, weasels, worms . . . I rejoice in the kinship. Even the caterpillar I can love, and the various vermin.

—THEODORE ROETHKE, from "Slug"

## THE PROBLEM

We cause our wild animal neighbors far more trouble than they cause us, as each day we invade thousands of acres of their territory and demolish their homes. Where their feeding and nesting grounds once thrived, are now our barren, crew-cut lawns.

According to Warren Schultz, in the *Chemical-Free Lawn* (Rodale Press, 1989), the average homeowner uses five-to-ten pounds of pesticides per lawn (amounting to 25–50 million pounds nationally).

## THE SOLUTION

Here are ways to help wildlings maintain *their* precious homes while keeping out of *yours:*

- Don't use pesticides in your yard. In addition to polluting the groundwater, lawn chemicals can endanger the songbird population by contaminating the worms they eat. No pesticide is safe for birds. Even those designed for the home will poison birds' water and food supplies.

- Leave a good part of your yard natural, with bushes and ground-cover. The more diverse your bushes, seeds, and berries, the greater variety of birds and small mammals you will attract and nurture. Cherish rare, huge, great-granddaddy den trees as well as brushy hedgerows—which are vital as homes for wildlings along the edges of woodlands and mowed areas. Two books that can help you attract and nurture wildlife are: *Attracting Backyard Wildlife: A Guide for Nature Lovers* by Bill Merilees (Stillwater, Minn.: Voyageur Press, 1989) and *Landscaping for Wildlife* by Carrol L. Henderson (St. Paul, Minn.: Minnesota Department of Natural Resources, 1987).

- Dead wood is ecological gold and crucial to kicking our pesticide habit. More than 150 species of birds and animals live in dead trees and/or feed on the insects there. Top off, rather than chop down, dead trees twelve inches or more in diameter. Fat dead logs, woody debris, and underbrush are also precious to wildlife. Before cutting any wood, check for nests and dens.

- Keep water in a birdbath and in a ground pan all year long. Use heating elements to keep them unfrozen in cold weather. Be sure neither is too close to a bush or other cover where a cat might hide.

- Install a martin house. Mosquitoes will disappear from your woodsy yard as elegant swifts, swallows, and purple martins sweep through the air.

- Lean planks or branches in uncovered window wells so creatures who may fall into them can climb out.

- If an animal has a nest of young in an unused part of your house and is doing no significant harm, leave the family alone for a few weeks until the youngsters are grown. They will probably then move out on their own.

- Squeals above your fireplace usually mean baby raccoons in your chimney. DON'T light a fire! They will move out in a few weeks. If you can't wait, put a radio tuned to loud talk or rock music in the fireplace and hang a mechanic's trouble light down the chimney. (Animals like their homes dark and quiet.) Leave these in place a few days, to give Mom time to find a new home and move her children. You might also hang a thick, knotted rope down the chimney, secured at the top, in case your tenant is not a raccoon and can't climb out unaided.

- Use this radio-light patience technique to evict animals from under the porch or in the attic as well, if necessary.
- Seal all entry places—*after* making sure no animals are inside. A mother animal will (justifiably) tear your roof apart if you seal her young inside.
- Use the above ways, rather than capturing and relocating an animal yourself or calling in "pest control agents" whose promises of humane destruction or relocation can be a fraud. Otherwise, you may be separating them from loved ones and food and water sources.
- Build a bat house. A bat consumes 3,000 or more mosquitoes and other insects nightly. Bats won't get in your hair and the chances of them being rabid are miniscule—less than that of your dog. Bats are responsible for up to 95 percent of the seed dispersal essential to the regeneration of tropical rain forests. For more information about bats, write: **Bat Conservation International,** P.O. Box 162603, Austin, TX 78716.
- If bats should enter your home, turn off all lights and open the doors and windows. If they still don't leave, they can be caught in a large jar or net and released outside. Wear gloves, since a frightened bat may bite. Then seal the point of entry, which may be as narrow as three-eighths of an inch.
- To certify your yard in the **National Wildlife Federation (NWF)** Backyard Wildlife Habitat Program, contact NWF at 1412 16th Street NW, Washington, DC 20036-2266.

# 15 STACK YOUR LIBRARY

Thus godlike sympathy grows and thrives and spreads far beyond the teachings of churches and schools, where too often the mean, blinding, loveless doctrine is taught that animals have neither mind nor soul, have no rights that we are bound to respect, and were made only for man, to be petted, spoiled, slaughtered, or enslaved.

—JOHN MUIR, "The Story of My Boyhood"

## THE PROBLEM

While most public and school library shelves bulge with "how-to" manuals and adventure stories about hunting and trapping, fur ranching, and dissection, they are sadly lacking in literature about animal rights and how we can curtail—and perhaps one day eliminate—the massive suffering involved in animal-based industries.

## THE SOLUTION

- PETA offers books, videos, fact sheets, vertical file materials, and colorful display boards free to school and public libraries. Have your librarian request them on library letterhead by writing LIBRARY PACK, **PETA,** P.O. Box 42516, Washington, DC 20015.
- Put up a library display. Most displays have to be reserved far in advance and must remain in place for a month. They give hundreds

of people a chance to absorb the information leisurely and comfortably. If you want to volunteer to set up a display, ask for permission from the librarian. (It's best that the library have the animal rights books and other literature in stock *before* setting up the display, since it will undoubtedly bring requests for materials.) Many libraries make displays using PETA's free animal rights library display board, and the relevant books, videos, and magazines.

- In conjunction with a display (or separately), some libraries offer handouts, including bibliographies, a filmography, a list of animal rights organizations, lists of companies that test on animals and those that don't, a summary of pending animal related legislation, lists of organizations that promote hunting and trapping and those that don't, and PETA fact sheets.

- Reserve a library room to present one or a series of talks and/or films on animal rights. These can include a question-and-answer period. Set up a literature table. Advance publicity can take the form of fliers at the library desk, posters on library and other public bulletin boards, call-ins to radio talk shows, newspaper ads and free newspaper listings on the weekly events pages. Many animal protection groups are happy to provide a speaker.

- Make sure your school or public library is receiving the magazines vital to the animal rights movement: *PETA News,* P.O. Box 42516, Washington, DC 20015, (301) 770-7444 (free); *The Animals' Voice Magazine,* P.O. Box 341347, Los Angeles, CA 90034, 1-800-82-VOICE; and **The Animals' Agenda,** P.O. Box 6809, Syracuse, NY 13217, (203) 452-0446.

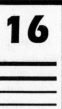

# 16 DEER EDITOR...

"Fool!" said my muse to me, "look in thy heart, and write."
—SIR PHILLIP SIDNEY, 1554–1586

## THE POWER OF THE PEN

With just a pen and paper, you can be a strong advocate for animals. Members of Congress receive more constituent mail about animal issues than about any other topic, except gun control and social security. An astounding 7,000–10,000 letters pour into congressional offices every week simply calling for improved treatment of animals on farms! Letter-writing campaigns aimed at businesses have helped prompt companies—including Walgreens, Spiegel, Hanes Hosiery, *Ladies Home Journal,* and Maidenform—to stop selling or giving away fur, and others—including Avon, Revlon, Crabtree & Evelyn, and Benetton—to stop testing cosmetics on animals. Effective letters to the editor have encouraged countless people to cut back on meat consumption, or to go to the theater instead of to an animal circus. Letters put animal protection issues before the public eye and catalyze debate.

## HOW TO WIELD IT

- Vow to write at least two letters a week: to elected officials, industry executives, newspaper and magazine editors, or whomever else you choose. *PETA News, The Animals' Voice Magazine,* and other animal rights publications can help you identify your new pen pals. Also, keep an eye on local news and events.

- To make the best impression, try to type your letter. Otherwise, print legibly, both to encourage the recipient to read your letter and to ensure that people are *able* to read it. (Needless to say, an illegible message is no message at all.) Make your letter brief, stating your objective early on. Always be polite and never threaten. Avoid personal attacks and be sure of your facts. Check your letter for grammar and spelling mistakes (if necessary, ask a friend to read it over and proofread it before mailing).

- When writing letters to the editor, follow the publication's instructions concerning length and personal information (such as full name, address, or telephone number). Add humor, if appropriate, but don't sacrifice the tone of a strong, serious letter just to add a punch line. If you have experience or a degree (such as an RN) applicable to the subject, mentioning it can give your letter a dash more credibility, but don't be afraid to speak out if you haven't any initials after your name.

- When writing a letter of complaint to a business, go to the top. Explain your reasons for objecting to the company's particular practice; don't launch into a tirade of "How can you be so cruel to innocent animals . . . !" Most people just don't realize the problem or have never stopped to think about it. *Always* suggest an alternative. If a radio station is giving away a fur coat, for instance, encourage the promotions manager to offer a trip or computer instead. Donnybrook Furlike Fashions of New York City has offered to replace real furs with faux furs in some promotions. A bar in Maryland agreed to substitute wind-up toys for real turtles in a scheduled race because of a customer's concerns and suggestion. Two sample letters to editors follow:

[Date]

Letters to the Editor
[Name of Newspaper]
[Address]

To the Editor:

Your article on cystic fibrosis patients ("Title of Article," date) was touching, but I take exception to one parent's remark about "vital" animal experiments. According to a representative of the Cystic Fibrosis Foundation, "No animal model exists for CF."

Instead of pouring billions (about seven of them, in fact) of dollars into making animals sick, we should study CF, AIDS, cancer, heart disease, and Alzheimer's noninvasively in human clinical studies, and we should spend more on programs that prevent disease—such as AIDS education, dietary recommendations, and improved prenatal care for the poor. Finally, we can use more relevant modern testing methods, such as epidemiological studies and computer programs that simulate human body functions.

We cannot realistically rely on animal tests to cure our ills, and our blind faith exacts a high price—in funding, in lives and in spirit.

Sincerely,

[Name, signed]
[Name, printed]
[Address]
[Phone number]

[Date]

Letters to the Editor
[Name of Newspaper]
[Address]

To the Editor:

The circus is in town, and advertisers are putting pressure on all of us to buy tickets early and avoid long lines. Long lines for what? To watch magnificent animals parade around in demeaning costumes, performing tricks that show none of the animals' beauty or intelligence but only the trainer's ability to dominate them.

The circus is a scam: visitors spend lots of money for tickets, but the animals pay the greatest price.

They spend most of their lives in cages; are dragged from town-to-town forty-eight weeks out of the year; and are forced to perform awkward, demeaning, and unnatural tasks. For *their* sakes, this year avoid the circus with its whips, muzzles, bars, hooks, and chains. If you want to see animals in action, try bird-watching.

Sincerely,

[Name, signed]
[Name, printed]
[Address]
[Phone number]

# 17 | SUPPORT YOUR LOCAL SHELTER

Knowing all truth is less than doing a little bit of good.
　　—**ALBERT SCHWEITZER,** *The Thoughts of Albert Schweitzer*

## THE PROBLEM AND THE POSSIBILITY

Just about every community has a shelter or pound overflowing with dogs and cats waiting to be adopted or for their families to find them. Either way, these animals are often scared and confused, and even though you can't take them all home with you, they would deeply appreciate your time, companionship, and resources.

Volunteering is a powerful tool for change. Helping minimize the impact of a seemingly overwhelming problem by making shelters more productive and less frightening places can be exceptionally fulfilling.

### The Scope of Need

- The Humane Society of the United States (HSUS) estimates that in 1983–1984 there were 900 private (humane society) shelters and 900 municipal shelters in the U.S. In 1990, the American Humane Association estimates that there are a total of 3,500 shelters in the U.S.
- HSUS estimates that animal shelters are currently handling approximately 12 million dogs and cats, and 1.5 million other animals, every year.

- There are approximately 200 wildlife rehabilitation centers in the United States, and the National Wildlife Rehabilitators Association has more than 700 members.

## THE SOLUTION

- Offer to clean the cats' quarters and play chase-the-string with the felines. Give them each some lap time for scratches behind the ears. Bring a *secure* cat harness and take the cats out for some sunshine on nice days.
- Donate blankets, newspapers, old towels, cat litter, and whatever else you can spare to make life more comfortable for the animals and less demanding on the shelter's funds. The more money your shelter saves on supplies, the more animals the facility can help.
- If your shelter has problems, help correct them. Rather than blaming the usually stressed and overworked employees for inadequacies, get involved in your community to upgrade your shelter. Roll up your own sleeves and form a "Friends of the Shelter" committee: lobby, raise funds and awareness, write to newspapers, do whatever it takes to improve the conditions for animals there.
- Volunteer to "ride along" to help load animals, carry crates, read the map, and provide an extra pair of hands. Such help makes a big difference to those who investigate cruelty charges, enforce animal protection and control laws, and confiscate abused animals. This experience will also help you talk from first-hand knowledge about the importance of spaying and neutering, the reasons why companion animals must not roam the streets unsupervised, and the ways in which animals suffer when neglected.
- Offer to take the dogs for walks one day a week or as often as you can. Play tug-of-war, bring treats (unsalted peanuts are a favorite for many dogs and, in the shell, peanuts give them more of a challenge). Let the animals know that they are worth something by giving them individual attention.
- Convince your local newspapers to run photos of the animals who are up for adoption at the shelter as a public service. Ask local television stations to help as well.

## Wild Animals Need Help, Too

Volunteer to help local wildlife rehabilitators nurse injured wildlife back
to good health and prepare them for release (your animal shelter should
have names and numbers). Volunteer your time to help in the round-
the-clock feeding of baby animals, who need to be fed and have their
bedding changed often. Wildlife rehabilitation operations, like shelters,
need soft bedding materials, newspapers, and other supplies. Most wildlife rehabilitation workers are good samaritans who aren't paid to help
sick, injured, and orphaned wildlife get back on their feet, and they
will welcome your assistance.

## RESOURCES

- **National Wildlife Rehabilitators Association (NWRA),** 708 Riverside Avenue So., Sartrell, MN 56377; (612) 252-3027. Call
  evenings and weekends only.
- **International Wildlife Rehabilitation Council (IWRC),** 4437
  Central Place, Suite B4, Suisan, CA 94585; (707) 864-1761.

# 18 | BE FISH FRIENDLY

There are three prerequisites for angling,
A hook, a line, and a stinker.
　—**JOHN BRYANT,** *Fettered Kingdoms*

Fish are so sensitive.
　—**CHO SHENG-GUNG,** Chinese acupuncturist, *Los Angeles Times,*
　　14 January 1989 (remark made after successfully treating
　　his ailing fishes with acupuncture)

The first rule in sport used to be fairness. But where is the fairness to
the fish? Animals are not footballs or tennis balls.
　—West German judge **HORST BRINKMANN,** upon fining angling
　　contest organizers for cruelty, 1988

Now I can look at you in peace; I don't eat you any more.
　—**FRANZ KAFKA,** remark reportedly made while
　　admiring fish in an aquarium

## THE PROBLEM

Whether they're swimming in a little glass tank "universe," dodging
plastic debris or crude oil, or struggling on a hook, fishes around the
world need our help.

　"Pet" fishes are sold in department stores (like Woolworth's) and
in pet shops, where they may be left in crowded tanks that are cleaned

infrequently; and live fishes to be eaten are sold in many grocery stores and fish markets. The capture of tropical salt-water species can wreak havoc on the fishes' natural surroundings; commercial fishermen in the Philippines and other Pacific islands hire young children to dive 100 feet or more to bang heavy rocks on vulnerable, precious coral reefs in order to chase fishes into nets, and others use explosives to stun the fish, making them easy to catch.

## Fish Facts

- People in the United States consume around 6.3 billion pounds of fish flesh annually.
- Around the world, close to 1,700 fishing vessels comb the oceans daily, leaving thousands of miles of plastic netting behind them, entangling and killing an estimated 100,000 marine mammals and at least 1 million birds annually. The boats dump garbage as well, choking and poisoning sea dwellers.
- The risk of food poisoning from eating fish is 25 times greater than from eating beef and 16 times greater than from eating poultry or pork.
- Some fishes have been found to have 9 million times the level of PCBs in their flesh as the level found in their home waters.
- Fishes use their tongues and lips like hands—to gather food and build nests—making sport fishing both debilitating and cruel. Fishes who are caught but thrown back become vulnerable to infection and predation. Some fishers spear the animals to kill them; others let them suffocate.
- In 1988, 58.6 million Americans spent $147 million on equipment to aid them in their grisly slaughter of more than a billion fishes all in the name of "sport."
- Because fishes don't show their pain in the same ways that mammals do, few people recognize fishing as the tragic carnage it is. Consider the following:

  • "Fish are very much 'animals' with well-developed brains and nervous systems and are as likely to feel pain as any other vertebrate" (Patty Mark, Animal Liberation, Melbourne, Australia).
  • A report published by Dutch scientists in 1988 gives evidence

that fish experience pain and fear to a degree comparable to human reactions of the kind. Measuring the amount of pain and fear experienced by fish hooked during angling, the scientists ascertained that "fish do experience fear and pain" (*Animals International,* 27 August 1988).

• Professor Frank Hird, eminent microbiologist of Melbourne University, has said, "The suffering that arises from neglecting biological justice in the fishing industry appalls me in the extreme" (on the 1974 ABC science program "Insight"), and "It is unthinkable for me that animals do not have pain receptors. They need them in order to learn to survive dangerous situations. The argument which says that vertebrates such as fish do not feel pain is an argument of convenience" (April 1985).

• Hooking is extremely painful to fish, as they have rich innervation in their lips, tongue, and mouth. "Playing" fish with a low-weight line causes fish great pain and stress, and veterinarians and scientists, as well as animal activists, have condemned the practice.

● Fish can be remarkably compassionate. A South African publication documented a case of a deformed Black Moor goldfish called "Blackie" and a Red Randi called "Big Red" who saved his life. Blackie had trouble swimming and for over a year Big Red came to his rescue daily. The publication stated: "Big Red constantly watches over his sick buddy, gently picking him up on his broad back and swimming him around the tank. When feeding time approaches and their keeper sprinkles goldfish food on the surface, Big Red immediately picks up Blackie and swims him to the surface, where both feed."

● An Australian government survey found that the two most highly regarded aspects of recreational fishing were to relax and unwind, 43 percent, and to be outdoors, 28 percent. Further down on the list was fishing for food, 7 percent (Patty Mark).

## THE SOLUTION

● Eat sea *vegetables* instead of sea *animals*. There are about ten different varieties of seaweeds commonly available in the U.S. from most health food stores. Use *nori* as a wrap for avocado and

cucumber sushi (contrary to popular myth, *sushi* does **not** mean
"raw fish"!); try *wakame* or *kombu* in soups; or toast *nori* as a
great salty snack. In restaurants, order pizza with mushrooms and
green peppers, not anchovies—and try it with marinara sauce instead of cheese!—or have a soy burger rather than a fish sandwich.
Eating vegetables, legumes, and fruits is the most compassionate
thing you can do for fishes.

- Check department stores and pet shops in your area for unclean
  tanks, fishes floating on top, and signs of crowding; an inch-long
  tropical fish requires at least 12 square inches of water surface to
  breathe comfortably; a 2-inch fish needs twice as much. Complain
  (politely) to management if you find problems, and put your complaint in writing to the store owners and local press. Refuse to
  patronize their stores until the problems are eliminated, preferably
  with the discontinuation of fish sales altogether.

- When relatives visit, steer them away from the local aquarium,
  which serves as a prison for fishes and marine mammals. Instead,
  show them your city's museums and historical sites. Follow the
  same policy when traveling.

# 19 FOR THE BIRDS: HELPING OUR FEATHERED FRIENDS

A Robin Red breast in a Cage
Puts all Heaven in a Rage.
   —WILLIAM BLAKE, "Auguries of Innocence"

So much for the idea that our feathered friends are all just bird brains.
   —DAVID STIPP, staff reporter of the *Wall Street Journal,*
      from "Einstein Bird Has Scientists Atwitter over Mental Feats"
      (profiling Alex, an African grey parrot who can
      name eighty of his favorite things, such as wool, walnut,
      and shower, and "can handle some simple abstractions
      as well as chimps and porpoises can")

The bird-catcher's trade and the bird-catcher's shop are alike full of horrors, and they are horrors which are due entirely to a silly fashion and a habit of callous thoughtlessness, not on the part of the ruffianly bird-catcher . . . who has to bear the burden of the odium attaching to these cruelties, but of the respectable customers who buy captured larks and linnets without the smallest scruple or consideration."
   —HENRY S. SALT, *Animals' Rights*

**FLIGHTY FACT:** Number of bird species sighted in Central Park since its establishment in 1858: 259 (*Harper's* "Index").

## THE PROBLEM

Who has not marveled at the grace and beauty of birds, and wished for wings? In cities, suburbs, and rural areas, on the oceans, mountains, and deserts, the omnipresence of birds of myriad species, colors, sizes, and shapes is a reminder of the diversity of life. The coos of city pigeons, the unearthly hoots of owls, and the warbles of thrushes are so much a part of the fabric of our ecosystem that birds seem indomitable; but in fact birds are highly vulnerable and in need of protection. Consider just a few of the many ways birds are endangered by human encroachment and abuse:

- *Pesticides and other chemicals:* DDT killed millions of birds before its use was stopped in the early 1970s. Bald eagles, whose eggshells DDT made too fragile to hatch, are only now returning from the brink of extinction. Granular carbofuran, a pesticide used since 1969 on corn and other crops (despite an EPA report concluding that a single granule can kill a bird), is blamed for the deaths of 2 million eagles, hawks, shrikes, sparrows, finches, and other birds each year. Pigeons, often considered a nuisance, are sometimes deliberately poisoned. Again, no pesticide is safe for birds: even ones designed for home use poison birds' water and food supplies.
- *Habitat destruction:* The single greatest threat to birds all over the world. Cities and suburbs expand, dams and reactors are built, destroying forests and waterways that birds need in order to survive. In the Pacific Northwest, 1,200 acres of ancient forest, critical to owls and eagles, are felled each week for timber. Fifty-three acres of South American rain forest—the winter homes of hundreds of species of songbirds and year-round homes to hundreds more— are leveled each *minute,* many of them to create cheap grazing land primarily to satisfy the North American demand for fast-food burgers.
- *"Sport" and entertainment:* Hunters maim and kill millions of geese, turkeys, pheasants, ducks, mourning doves, and other birds each year. Hunters also shoot predators—eagles, owls, hawks— who compete with them for "game," even though some of these predator birds are protected by federal law, at least on paper.

Community pigeon shoots (like the notorious Hegins, Pennsylvania, annual festival and shoot, in which local children wring the necks of the fallen, injured birds) are no fun for the birds they slaughter. Fishing, too, takes its toll on shorebirds who become tangled in lines (often fatally) and caught on hooks.

- *The exotic bird trade:* One-quarter of a million or more parrots, macaws, cockatoos, fragile hummingbirds, and other "exotic" birds are smuggled into the United States and other countries annually—often in tandem with drugs—to be sold to pet shops and dealers, who in turn sell them at premium prices (up to $100,000). These intelligent birds, many of whom pair for life and who can live 60 to 80 years or longer, are stuffed into false-bottom suitcases; sewn into the lining of coats; jammed into pipes, hair rollers or gutted auto parts, their beaks taped shut. The 50 to 75 percent mortality rate from this treatment only increases their rarity and, hence, their selling price. Further facts:

  • Approximately 140 parrots are smuggled from Mexico into the United States every day. Five to 10 birds die for each bird who arrives in the U.S. alive.
  • Wing-shooting (shooting birds' wings with pellets to wound and render them flightless for easy capture) is still common; as it requires good aim, more birds are killed than wounded.

## WHAT YOU CAN DO TO HELP BIRDS

- Plant trees for nesting and berry bushes and other plants attractive to birds for food to help compensate for wide-spread destruction of bird habitats. Virginia creeper (a perennial vine), white oak, and eastern red cedar trees provide food and cover for wildlings; while coralberry, honeysuckle, and serviceberry shrubs are primarily a source of nectar and food for birds and other animals. Nest boxes and feeding tables will also encourage birds to settle (and, as an added benefit to both you and them, eat the insects attacking your plants). For more information on bird-friendly landscaping, read *Trees, Shrubs and Vines for Attracting Birds,* by

Richard M. Degraaf and Gretchin M. Witman (Amherst: University of Massachusetts Press, 1979).

• Caution: poinsettia and mistletoe are poisonous to birds!
• Install a birdbath with a coil heater in your yard, as well as a bird feeder (but be sure to keep them maintained all winter and spring—birds come to depend on them).

- Cap your chimney; this simple step can save the lives of birds (and squirrels) who might otherwise fall in.
- Birds fly into windows (and can suffer concussions or mandible or eye damage) either because they see their own reflections and mistake them for "intruders," because they are attracted to something inside, or because the sky is reflected in the window. To prevent this, place hawk silhouettes, wind chimes, or streamers in the window, and close drapes or blinds whenever possible.
- If a bird enters your house, wait until dark, then open a window and put a light outside it. Turn out all house lights, and the bird should fly out to the light.
- *Never, never, never* buy a caged bird. Birds are flock animals, not loners, who need room to fly. Wild birds make sad, lonely, and sometimes dangerous "pets." Captive-bred birds are more docile, but breeders must constantly introduce new genes ("new blood") from wild-caught birds, so even buying only captive-bred birds supports the wild-caught bird trade.
- Discourage pet shops from carrying birds. Work to get your city or town to pass an ordinance banning the sale of birds. Complain to the managers and presidents of hotels and resorts that keep caged birds.
- *Never* use poison or sticky repellent caulk to control pigeons, starlings, or other birds. A stretched-out Slinky, nailed to a board and placed on a window ledge or roof, will keep birds from roosting. If your city or town poisons birds, urge them to substitute humane forms of control (write to **PETA** or **HSUS** for a fact sheet).
- At weddings, throw bird seed instead of rice (which can swell in birds' stomachs, proving fatal to them).
- Let the U.S. Forest Service know that you're one taxpayer who believes wilderness areas should benefit their denizens, not special interests like hunters and loggers.

- Remove kite string from trees—birds can get tangled in it and die.
- Don't buy hats or anything else with feathers; birds may have been killed for their plumage. Also avoid down, which is often plucked from live geese.

## 20 | BE A MOBILE ACTIVIST

Nothing is more powerful than an individual acting out of his conscience, thus helping to bring the collective conscience to life.
—**NORMAN COUSINS,** *Human Options*

### THE PROBLEM

The motto of the activist should be that of the Scout: *Semper Paratus* (''Be prepared''). Too often, we leave a situation saying, ''If only I had . . .''

Movements for social change thrive on visibility, but usually can't afford large advertising budgets. So, the ''Army of the Kind'' must outfit itself with pamphlets and paraphernalia designed to turn heads and change minds. You'll find it helpful to stock up your cars, purses, and backpacks with materials designed to raise people's consciousness.

### THE SOLUTION

- If you have a car, use it to send a message to thousands of people a year (and don't wait until your car is old and rusted!). Use:

  • *Bumper stickers.* ''Love Animals, Don't Eat Them''(1),* ''Fur Is Dead''(1), ''Meat Is Murder''(1), ''Save the Chimps''(1),

*Number in parentheses indicates place where item can be purchased; see ''Sources'' at end of chapter.

72

"Support Your Right to Arm Bears"(2), "Conserve a Hunter: Harvest One Today"(2), "Animals—It's Their World, Too"(3), "Peace Begins in the Kitchen: Go Vegetarian"(4), "Vegetarians Are Sprouting Up All Over"(5), and many more available from animal protection groups.

• *License plates.* NO MINK, BAN FUR, GOVEGIE, SPAY, R U VEG, EATTOFU, LUVRATS, PIG LIB, RAT LIB.

• *Hood, roof, side-panel messages.* EVERY FUR HURTS, STOP ANIMAL TESTING, IT TAKES 40 DUMB ANIMALS TO MAKE A FUR COAT—BUT ONLY ONE TO WEAR IT, CHOOSE A LIVING EARTH: GO VEGETARIAN.

• Stock your car with an animal rescue kit that includes: nonperishable food for hungry strays; a collapsible cardboard cat carrier (available from some "pet" supply stores and shelters); a long, light (canvas or nylon) leash—to be made into a loop collar for capturing dogs and cats; a bandage for a muzzle (an injured dog may snap or bite); a string bag to transport an unfamiliar cat (allowing her/him to walk, while you still maintain control); and *don't forget* to take along the emergency phone numbers of veterinarians and shelters/humane societies in your area.

• Carry a camera in order to thoroughly record any instances of animal abuse. Your case will always be stronger if recorded on film.

• Carry leaflets and brochures supporting spaying or opposing dissection in your glove compartment, purse, and/or bag. Always leave a few in laundromats, doctors' and dentists' offices, on public transportation, and in taxis, church pews, restaurants, and department-store dressing rooms. Replace Beef and Dairy Council and hunting propaganda with animal rights literature.

• Carry seasonal literature. In the winter, don't go without anti-fur cards to place in the pockets of fur coats on store racks or mannequins or to hand to fur-coat wearers, e.g., "Here's what the people who sell fur don't want you to see," or "We'd like you to meet someone who used to wear fur"(1). In the summer, carry pamphlets to place on cars in which animals have been left in the heat.

• Print up or handwrite and have available tags to place on the collars of or around the necks of dogs who have been left outside shops by their guardians, alerting them to the danger of having the dog stolen for research or dogfights (sample text: "I could have stolen your dog for laboratory research. Please don't leave him/her unattended.").

- On the shelf next to products manufactured by companies that still test on animals, place "Warning: Cruelly Tested on Animals"(1) signs. Inside menus, place warning cards that clarify menu items such as "Animal Flesh."
- If you see calf on the menu when you eat out leave "No Veal This Meal"(3) information cards. Carry vegetarian and vegan (fully vegetarian) recipe cards (1,6) to hand to restaurant managers and staff—they are also the perfect answer to "Doubting Thomases" you meet along the way who ask, "But what do you eat?"
- Order and carry with you a self-inking stamp with an animal rights message. Where appropriate, you can stamp such messages as "ANIMALS HAVE RIGHTS" and "GO VEGETARIAN."

## SOURCES

1. **PETA,** P.O. Box 42516, Washington, DC 20015; (301) 770-7444.
2. **The Fund for Animals,** 850 Sligo Avenue, Silver Spring, MD 20910; (301) 585-2591.
3. **The Humane Society of the United States,** 2100 L Street NW, Washington, DC 20037; (202) 452-1100.
4. **Vegan Street,** P.O. Box 5525, Rockville, MD 20855; 1-800-422-5525.
5. **The Vegetarian Resource Group,** P.O. Box 1463, Baltimore, MD 21203; (301) 366-VEGE.
6. **The Physicians Committee for Responsible Medicine (PCRM),** P.O. Box 6322, Washington, DC 20015; (202) 686-2210.

# 21 | IT'S RAINING CATS AND DOGS

People who let their dogs and cats have litters in order to show their children the "miracle of birth" should come witness the "miracle of death" performed in the back rooms of animal shelters all over the country.

—**PHYLLIS WRIGHT,** director of sheltering, Humane Society of the United States.

## THE PROBLEM

What's happening to our best friends should never happen even to our worst enemies. With an estimated 80 to 100 million cats and dogs in this country already, 3,000 to 5,000 more puppies and kittens are born every *hour* in the United States—far more than can ever find good homes. Unwanted animals are dumped at the local pound or abandoned in woods and on city streets, where they suffer from starvation, lack of shelter and veterinary care, and abuse. Most die from disease, starvation, and mistreatment, or, *if they're lucky,* are "put to sleep" forever at an animal shelter. Some will be shunted through a series of homes and heartbreaks (how do you explain to a dog why her family abandoned her?).

## ... Is Overwhelming

- A female dog reaches sexual maturity at about 6 months of age and comes into heat twice a year thereafter. She may give birth to a litter of puppies every 6 months. Female cats can be even more prolific, reaching sexual maturity at about the same age as dogs, but coming into heat every 2 to 3 weeks, from February until late summer. One female cat may have as many as 3 or 4 litters a year, with as many as 6 kittens per litter.
- Just one female cat and her offspring can produce 48 more cats in just 16 months; and one female dog and her offspring can be responsible for the birth of 4,372 dogs in 7 years!
- There are approximately 56 million cats today in the U.S.; 15 to 25 million of them are homeless. For every cat fortunate enough to find a home, 12 others eke out an existence in alleys and sewers. Statistics for dogs are nearly as grim.
- Fewer than 15 percent of all impounded dogs and cats nationwide are re-homed. The rest are either destroyed or, in areas where pound seizure is legal, sold or given to laboratories.
- In one of the great tragic ironies of our disposable society, the remains of animals killed on highways and in vet clinics, laboratories, and pounds are often *rendered* (boiled in huge vats) into ingredients used to make soaps, candles, and even dog and cat food.

## THE SOLUTION

- Neuter and spay! Many municipalities and humane societies have low-cost spay/neuter programs. Even paying top dollar for this once-in-a-lifetime surgery beats the expense and trouble of dealing with unwanted litters.
- Work with your local shelters and legislators to start a low-cost spay/neuter clinic. In San Mateo County, California, the number of animals handled by the Peninsula Humane Society dropped by 39 percent from 1973 to 1974 when the county did just that.
- Never patronize pet shops and breeders—they contribute to dog

and cat overpopulation. The animals at your local shelter have personality, charm, and looks. *You* could be their lifeline.

## What's the Procedure for Spaying and Neutering?

Spaying or neutering is surgical sterilization. Spaying of females involves the removal of the uterus and the ovaries, and usually requires an overnight stay at the veterinarian's office. Neutering of males is done by removing the testicles, and dogs and cats can usually go home the same day. Responsible animal shelters presterilize adopted animals or require those who adopt animals to spay or neuter them. Spaying and neutering makes animals much less likely to roam in search of a breeding partner or fight for one. It also helps prevent mammary and testicular cancers. Altered males don't climb over or dig under fences to pursue females in heat across town, and they don't spray furniture or drapes.

## RESOURCES

- **Humane Society of the United States (HSUS)**, 2100 L Street NW, Washington, DC 20037, (202) 452-1100, and your local humane society.
- **Friends of Animals'** low-cost spay/neuter hotline: 1-800-631-2212.
- **PETA** has spay/neuter pamphlets available for distribution.

# 22 | **THE FLAP ABOUT FLIPPER**

Perhaps in some way I owe my medals to the dolphins. In their trusting and playful way, they taught me the subtleties of swimming technique.

> —**MATT BIONDI,** Olympic gold medal winner,
> appealing to Congress to strengthen
> the Marine Mammal Protection Act

I wish to tell you what we have learned of a group of uninhibited nudists who have never worn clothes. . . . They have big brains and bright minds . . .

> —**DR. JOHN LILLY,** noted dolphin researcher,
> in one of his many lectures on dolphins

## THE PROBLEM

Dolphins: graceful, enigmatic, and revered—and the object of endless controversy. When this country's three major tuna companies, responsible for 75 percent of the tuna sold in the United States, announced an end to their purchase of tuna from fishing companies that use seine nets (which, since the early 1960s, have killed over a quarter of a million dolphins annually), environmentalists and animal rights advocates celebrated.*

While dolphins in the oceans may be a little safer now thanks to

---

*However, because official observers on tuna fishing vessels are human, and therefore neither infallible nor able to be everywhere at once, and because the tuna suffer as well, a continuing boycott of tuna products can still help many animals, including the dolphins.

consumer action (and company re-action), dolphins in captivity continue to suffer. Ric O'Barry, who trained the dolphin Flipper for the television show, became an animal rights advocate when the famous mammal died in his arms of the loneliness and stresses of captive life. Flipper was just a youngster. According to O'Barry, "the average age of death of a captive dolphin is 5.8 years." (The average natural lifespan of free-roaming dolphins is 25 years.)

- Dolphin "swim-with" programs are being introduced at more and more hotels across the country. Hotel guests pay $50 or so to swim with a dolphin who has been captured (or bred) and is kept for the purpose of entertainment. In 1989, in Florida alone, there were 143 captive dolphins on display, many of them in swim-with programs. The people who swim with them are not required to have any understanding of dolphins or other animals, and some people have been injured or frightened by the advances of sexually frustrated male dolphins. Humans are sometimes intoxicated or sick, which makes them potentially dangerous to the dolphins who are susceptible to human disease, especially when their immune systems are depressed by the stress of confinement.

- Although profiteers' publicists contend that dolphin and whale shows at Sea World and other marine parks teach viewers about animals, the overriding image is one of frivolity and artificiality, teaching nothing about the natural dignity and behavior of these intelligent individuals or the plight of animals whose home is being trashed by human industry.

- Former U.S. Navy dolphin trainers like Rick Trout are speaking out publicly against the military conscription of these intelligent and peace-loving mammals into involuntary service, where they are trained in maneuvers hazardous to themselves and to humans. Forced to hunt mines, retrieve spent torpedoes, and "deactivate" potential human saboteurs of barges and nuclear submarines, dolphins have become the military's favorite disposable soldiers. The navy has used dolphins, sea lions, and beluga whales in classified programs since the 1960s and is now placing .45-caliber guns on the dolphins' snouts and training them to ram the devices, which trigger on impact, into "enemy frogmen." In 1988, the Seattle *Post-Intelligencer* reported that 13 dolphins in training for the navy's marine mammal program had died during a two-year period.

According to the report, nearly half of them suffered from depression, loss of appetite, stomach ulcers, and severe stress before their deaths.

## Dolphin Documentation

- Dolphins and whales become too depressed to breed well in captivity, so the introduction of dolphin swim programs and the expansion of aquariums and marine parks mean the capture of free-roaming ocean dolphins. Removing a dolphin from her/his family (or pod) and transporting the animal to an unfamiliar location is highly traumatic and amounts to sentencing the animal to prison. What confinement does to mammals who navigate by sonar is frightening to contemplate.
- In the ocean, dolphins, who weigh 300–500 pounds, typically travel 40 miles a day at speeds up to 35 miles per hour. At Sea World, 16 dolphins share with 2 beluga whales a pool that is only 80 feet long and 13 feet deep.
- At the National Aquarium in Baltimore, dolphins spend 98 percent of their time in the parts of their tanks farthest from spectators. Three bottlenose dolphins there developed ulcers in response to their inability to escape the crowds of people gathering to look at them, and one died.
- The abuses dolphins have suffered at the hands of humans haven't stopped them from helping their awkward fellow earth-dwellers. In January of 1988, dolphins guided three ship-wrecked sailors to shore through shark-infested, turbulent waters a mile off South Africa's east coast. The dolphins reportedly stayed with the men throughout their two-hour ordeal. Jacques Cousteau has documented a relationship between the people of Mauritania and dolphins, in which dolphins brought people fish.
- When the Dalai Lama won the Nobel Peace Prize in 1989, 18 Tibetan monks celebrated by chanting to dolphins at the Miami Seaquarium. Marine scientists said the sound waves produced by the chanting were pleasing to the dolphins, who kept their heads out of the water, some tilting their heads to the side to hear better.

## THE SOLUTION

- When you make hotel reservations, tell your travel agent that you will not stay in any place that features a dolphin swim program. When you visit cities with marine parks or aquariums, put other sights on your agenda.
- In your hometown, keep informed about the activities of your local aquarium. If aquarium officials are considering an expansion or want to add (or replace) a dolphin to their "stock," protest vigorously—to aquarium officials, to Fish & Wildlife officials, to local legislators, and in letters to area publications. Suggest a display of animal models, aquatic plants, and coral reefs instead. Write to **The Cousteau Society** (see "Resources" at end of chapter) and ask about the Cousteau Oceanic Park in Paris, which exhibits models of sea creatures enhanced by special effects and audio-visual processes to create an underwater environment. Other attractions include a theater program that simulates an ocean descent and a walk-in model of a pregnant blue whale.
- Write to the **U.S. Department of Fisheries,** 5010 Overlook Avenue SW, Washington, DC 20032, and your congressperson to ask for a ban on any capture and confinement of marine mammals. When enough people request action, the dolphins will be freed.
- Exploiting dolphins for our national defense endeavors is ethically indefensible. Humans must take responsibility for their own wars. In 1989, a coalition of fifteen animal rights and environmentalist groups sued the U.S. Navy to stop a project in which dolphins are trained to detect submarines entering Puget Sound. Write your congressional representatives asking them to cut off funds for military deployment of dolphins.

## RESOURCES

- **Sea Shepherd Society,** P.O. Box 7000-S, Redondo Beach, CA 90277; (213) 373-6979.
- **Save the Dolphins Project (Earth Island Institute),** 300 Broadway, Suite 28, San Francisco, CA 94133; (415) 788-3666.

- **The Cousteau Society,** 930 West 21st Street, Norfolk, VA 23517; (804) 627-1144.
- **Animal Welfare Institute,** P.O. Box 3650, Washington, DC 20007; (202) 337-2333.

# 23 FUR IS DEAD

Fur used to turn heads, now it turns stomachs.
                              —RUE McCLANAHAN


## THE PROBLEM

The good news is, the fur industry feels trapped. Since vigorous anti-fur campaigns have begun, fur trade journals report that the "harvest" of wild animals for fur has dropped as much as 80 percent. Harrods of London announced in March 1990 that its fur salon would close, and in April 1990 Spiegel dropped fur from its catalogue. Leaders in the fashion industry, including Giorgio Armani, Bill Blass, and Norma Kamali, have pledged never again to work with fur.

The bad news is, every year approximately 44 million animals are still killed for the production of fur. For every "target" animal trapped, three "trash" animals (e.g., cats, dogs, deer, and birds) are killed. One 40-inch-long wild mink coat can represent 60 "target" animals and 180 unintended victims. So for each fur bought, up to 240 animals can lose their lives, needlessly suffering a combined total of up to 3,600 hours in traps. That's more than *5 months* of agony per coat.


## Trapping Truths

- Most fur garments (about 74 percent) are derived from animals killed by trappers. Every year millions of coyotes, foxes, raccoons, lynxes, rabbits, bobcats, muskrats, sables, opossums, and other animals find themselves locked in spring-loaded leg-hold traps—which are now banned in at least 70 countries and in Florida, Rhode Island, and New Jersey.

- The shock suffered by animals when caught in a leg-hold trap is, as British behaviorist Dr. Desmond Morris has explained, "difficult for us to conceive, because it is a shock of total lack of understanding of what has happened to them. They are held, they cannot escape, their response very often is to bite at the metal with their teeth, break their teeth in the process and sometimes even chew through the leg that is being held in the trap." Up to one-in-four trapped animals (around 2 million per year) chews off his or her own leg or foot to escape, but those who drag themselves away from the traps often die later of blood loss, predation (because they are no longer quick enough to escape), or infection. Trapped animals who do not die before the trapper arrives (often *days* later) are shot, beaten, or stomped to death; trappers are taught to stand on the animal's chest and yank the hind legs out, crushing the lungs.

- The number of animals needed to make a 40-inch coat varies, depending on the animal used: 15 beavers, 16 coyotes, 18 lynxes, 45 opossums, 50 muskrats. (Multiply by three to get the total number of animals killed per coat.)

- Trapping is not an effective tool for "wildlife management," contrary to fur-industry propaganda. Trapping disrupts wildlife populations by killing healthy animals needed to keep the species strong, and populations are further damaged when the parents of young animals are killed.

## Fur Farms (Ranch-"Razed" Fur)

- Animals on fur farms live their short lives in wire-mesh cages, victims of stress, fear, and self-mutilation. In the interest of profit, animals are dispatched by the cheapest methods possible, which are usually also the most crude and cruel, e.g., anal electrocution, poisoning with weed killer, and suffocation.

- Only 24 percent of fur coats made in the U.S. and Canada come from captive-raised animals. There are approximately 970 mink farms, 3,000 fox farms, and 750 chinchilla farms, plus a few dozen farms that breed and slaughter rabbits and beavers.

- The fur industry, which has been unable to report a rise in profits since 1987, still sells $1.5 billion worth of dead-animal skins per year.

- Foxes are kept in wire-mesh cages only 2.5 feet square, with up to 4 animals per cage. Minks and other species are generally kept in 1-foot-by-3-foot cages, again with up to 4 animals per cage.

- In 1987, U.S. mink farmers reported that 450,000 animals died of heat stress on their farms.

- South Korea has become one of the leading fur manufacturing countries of the world. In 1987, its exports to the United States, Europe, and Japan amounted to $115 million and continue to rise.


## THE SOLUTION

- *Don't wear fur,* and avoid toys and other items made with fur. If you are attached to the fur "look," or know someone who is, give yourself or your friend a fake. "Faux fur" has become a fashion statement among many designers who are opposed to the cruelty real fur represents.

- If you already have a fur, send it to **PETA** or to another animal protection organization as a tax-deductible donation. It will be useful for educational projects such as anti-fur demonstrations and displays.

- Don't shop in department stores with fur boutiques or in stores that carry fur clothing, accessories, or toys. Write to or speak with the store managers to let them know you oppose the inhumane treatment of animals.

- Write or call businesses that use furs as contest prizes and ask them to consider the animals and stop promoting cruelty.

- Get fur out of *Vogue*—a fashion magazine in need of a compassion make-over. Write editor-in-chief Anna Wintour, 350 Madison Avenue, New York, NY 10017. Let the editors of any other magazines featuring furs know that you don't like their style.

- Support anti-fur legislation, and write your legislators asking them to do the same. Some legislation would ban leg-hold traps, other bills attempt to ban the sale of fur altogether. For current information on congressional bills, contact the **National Alliance for Animal Legislation,** P.O. Box 75116, Washington, DC 20015, (703) 684-0654, or the **Society for Animal Protective Legislation,** P.O. Box 3719, Georgetown Station, Washington, DC 20007, (202) 337-2334.

- Join rallies and demonstrations to help teach others that trapping and fur "ranching" are destructive practices stemming from greed, not glamour.
- Donate to a local campaign action group or national organizations like **HSUS** and **PETA** to help fund anti-fur billboards and ads.
- Order a **PETA** Fur Action Pack ($15 donation, includes PETA membership) or Video Fur Action Pack ($25). The Fur Action Pack includes a T-shirt, bumper sticker, fact sheets, anti-fur cards to educate fur wearers, and fliers to start your own anti-fur campaign. The Video Pack includes the same, plus an "Exporting Cruelty" video, narrated by Bea Arthur.

# 24 | WINNERS DON'T EAT WEINERS

I have a friendly feeling towards pigs generally, and consider them the most intelligent of beasts. . . . I also like his attitudes towards all other creatures, especially man. . . . He views us from a totally different, a sort of democratic standpoint as fellow citizens and brothers, and takes for granted, or grunted, that we understand his language, and without servility or insolence he has a natural, pleasant, camerados-all or hail-fellow-well-met air with us.''

> —Naturalist **W. H. HUDSON**, *Book of a Naturalist* (as quoted in John Robbins' *Diet for a New America*)

## THE PROBLEM

Pigs are among the least understood and most persecuted of all animals. Personable and clean (if allowed room to escape their own waste), their intelligence exceeds that of our close companion, the dog. Yet pigs spend their much-shortened lives in bleak factory buildings, suffering abuses that would create a national outcry if inflicted on ''man's best friend.'' Eighty-five million pigs are slaughtered annually for U.S. dinnertime fare, like pork chops. Far away from a mud wallow or the sounds and smells of the forests and jungles that were once their homes, 70 to 90 percent of the pigs raised for pork, bacon, and sausage are tethered by the neck in metal and concrete pens on factory farms before being trucked, sometimes great distances, to the slaughterhouse.

- *Breeders:* "The breeding sow should be thought of, and treated, as a valuable piece of machinery whose function is to pump out baby pigs like a sausage machine" (I. J. Taylor, Export Development Manager, Wall's Meat Company).

  "Farrowing operations" is the industry term for breeding factories, whose aim is to churn out as many pigs per litter and as many litters per year as possible. Hundreds of sows are fertilized either by boars (on what pig farmers call "rape racks") or by artificial insemination. Farmers often use large doses of hormones to ensure constant fertility. Once pregnant, a sow is warehoused for 15 weeks in a gestation building, where she is chained and confined in a small, dark metal stall called an "iron maiden" and is fed only once every 2 or 3 days. Two-to-three weeks after giving birth, the young pigs are sold en masse to "finishing operations" (pig "fattening" factories), and the sow is ready to be reimpregnated.

- *Feeders:* "Forget the pig is an animal. Treat him like a machine in a factory. Schedule treatments like you would lubrication. Breeding like the first step in an assembly line. And marketing like the delivery of finished goods" (J. Brynes, *Hog Farm Management*).

  Feeders raise the piglets in confinement cages stacked three or four tiers high—having already cut off their tails (to prevent neurotic tail-biting, behavior that results from close confinement), notched their ears, clipped their needle teeth, and castrated the males, all without anesthesia. At twenty weeks, they are shipped to slaughter.

## Still Wish You Were a Weiner?

In "Watching the Animals" (*Harper's,* March 1970), Richard Rhodes wrote, of the last hours of factory-farmed pigs' lives: "Before they reach their end, the pigs get a shower, a real one. Water sprays from every angle to wash the farm off them. Then they begin to feel crowded. The pen narrows like a funnel; the drivers behind urge the pigs forward, until one at a time they climb onto the moving ramp. . . . Now they scream, never having been on such a ramp, smelling the smells they smell ahead. . . . It was a frightening experience, seeing their fear, seeing so many of them go by, it had to remind me of things no one wants to be reminded of anymore, all mobs, all death marches, all mass murders and executions.''

- ''Modern'' pigs, bred for more meat, develop painful foot and leg lesions because they can't support their extra weight.
- Because of stress, some factory pigs ''freeze-up'': they become so afraid that they cannot move, even to eat or drink. Others remain in constant, panicked motion, a neurotic perversion of their instinct to escape.
- Approximately 30 percent of all pork products are contaminated with toxoplasmosis, a disease caused by parasites that can be passed on to consumers.
- Twenty-three percent of pigs (24 million per year) die before reaching slaughter age in the United States, according to the U.S. Department of Agriculture. Most die from respiratory disease brought on by enclosed housing and aggravated by crowding and stress. An additional 416,000 pigs die from ''shipping stress'' each year on the way to the slaughterhouse.

## THE SOLUTION

. . . is much less complex than the problem: don't eat pig flesh in any form, including ham, bacon, sausages, and hotdogs.

- Beware of pig by-products such as lard, which is often used in commercial refried beans and french fries.
- Try an alternative; some are eerily close to the ''real thing.'' Check at your local health food store for ''Tofu Pups,'' vegetarian hot dogs distributed by **Lightlife Foods,** P.O. Box 870, Greenfield, MA 01302, (413) 774-6001; **Spring Creek Soy Dairy**'s ''Soysage,'' Spencer, WV 25276; and Baco's Salad Sprinkles made from texturized vegetable protein. Or make barbequed tofu in a rich (vegetarian!) sauce. At a contest for the best ribs in Chicago, vegetarians challenged the judges with Barbequed Kofu Ribs, a recipe calling for well-seasoned wheat gluten ''ribs,'' baked or

broiled until browned and crisp, and then braised or baked in a flavorful barbecue sauce. (For a copy of the recipe, send $2 and a note to *Vegetarian Times,* P.O. Box 570, Oakpark, IL 60301, and specify that you want to know how to make "Barbequed Kofu Ribs" from *Vegetarian Times,* July 1986.)

# 25 BRINGING ANIMALS INTO THE FOLD

There is no religion without love, and people may talk as much as they like about their religion, but if it does not teach them to be good and kind to other animals as well as humans, it is all a sham.

—ANNA SEWELL, *Black Beauty*

## BACKGROUND

Religion, one of whose tenets traditionally has been reverence for life (including respect for animals and the earth), is one of the strongest and most influential institutions in our society, and is a guiding force for hundreds of millions of people. What an impact organized religion can have when it embraces concern for *all* animals; yet what is preached often may not be what is practiced.

Virtually every religious tradition, from Christianity to Jainism and from Hinduism to Judaism, extolls the virtues of compassion and mercy. Many religious leaders and theologians, including Mohandas K. Gandhi, Dr. Albert Schweitzer, and the Reverend Norman Vincent Peale, have fervently argued the rights of other-than-human beings and the importance of making the ethical treatment of *all* animals a theological priority. This is a powerful and significant heritage.

## WHAT YOU CAN DO

- Make your church or synagogue a place of all-encompassing compassion. Rev. Carolyn Michael Riley, a minister in New York, declared her church a fur-free zone and delivers sermons on adopting a vegan lifestyle. Her church library houses animal rights' books and pamphlets as well as displays of cruelty-free cosmetics and household products.
- Watch and share the film *We Are All Noah,* a twenty-nine-minute documentary on religious perspectives of animal welfare and rights, with family, friends, and religious groups. Available for $50 (U.S.) postage-paid from **The Culture and Animals Foundation,** 3509 Eden Croft Drive, Raleigh, NC 27612; (919) 782-3739.
- To get a free booklet on religion, animals, and nature protection, send a self-addressed, stamped envelope to the **Interfaith Council for the Protection of Animals and Nature (ICPAN)**, 2841 Colony Road, Ann Arbor, MI 48104, an organization dedicated to persuading clergy, religious leaders, and laypeople of all faiths and denominations that their help is needed if we are going to stop the ecological destruction of our planet.
- Vegetarian seders are now held in cities around the world at Passover. Contact **Jewish Vegetarians of North America,** P.O. Box 1463, Baltimore, MD 21203, (301) 366-8343, for *No Cholesterol Passover Recipes* with one hundred vegan Passover recipes for $5.00. According to Steven Rosen, in *Food for the Spirit,* the first ten generations of Jews (from Adam to Noah) were frugivorous vegetarians.

## RESOURCES

- **International Network for Religion and Animals (INRA):** 2913 Woodstock Avenue, Silver Spring, MD 20910; (301) 565-9132. Objective: to bring religious principles to bear upon humanity's attitude toward the treatment of nonhuman animals. INRA is ecumenical and international in its outreach.

- **Jews for Animal Rights:** 255 Humphrey Street, Marblehead, MA 01945; (617) 631-7601. Provides education about animal abuse, and influences Jewish communities to change attitudes and behavior. Illuminates role of Jewish people and their relationship to animals. Free literature, periodical newsletter, no membership dues.
- **Unitarian Universalists for Ethical Treatment of Animals (UFETA):** 230 W. 78th Street, New York, NY 10024. UFETA works with over 1,000 congregations to introduce the issue of animal rights and to initiate observances on church calendars (Meat-Out Day, World Day for Animals in Laboratories, World Prayer Week for Animals, etc.); encourages congregations nationwide to adopt resolutions for the rights of animals and incorporate the philosophy and language into sermons; sponsors a major animal rights speaker every June at the General Assembly to address the over 5,000 attendees who are mostly religious educators, ministers, etc. (Membership: $15 supporting; $25 sustaining; $40 organization. Contributors receive a newsletter twice a year in addition to several other mailings.)

# 26 | HALT THE HUNT

You ask people why they have deer heads on the wall. They always say, "Because it's such a beautiful animal." There you go. I think my mother's attractive, but I have photographs of her.
    —ELLEN DeGENERES, "On Location: Women of the Night"

The squirrel that you kill in jest, dies in earnest.
    —HENRY D. THOREAU, *Familiar Letters*

## THE PROBLEM

From the Mojave Desert to the woods of Maine, a small but violent minority known as American hunters invade public and private lands each year to kill animals for fun and profit. Approximately 15 million hunters—only 7 percent of the U.S. population—engage in annual offensives against wildlife, the environment, and people who get in their way. Their 200 million annual victims include deer, bears, moose, rabbits, ducks, geese, squirrels, and other wildlife, as well as dogs, cats, cows, occasional hikers, and quite a few fellow hunters (hunting catalogues even sell camouflaged toilet paper to help hunters avoid being mistaken for white-tailed deer!). Hunters also leave behind many wounded and crippled animals; it is estimated that, for every animal a hunter kills and recovers, at least two wounded animals die slowly and painfully of blood loss, infection or starvation, and those who don't die often suffer from disabling injuries.

Natural predators of the species that the hunters themselves wish to kill are victims of either the annual massacre called "game management" or the $30 million tax-funded "predator control" program. Millions of animals, ranging from wolves and mountain lions to badgers and owls, lose their lives to federally subsidized squeezes of the trigger.

While natural predators keep their prey species strong by killing only the sickest and weakest members, human pleasure hunters seek out and destroy the strongest and most fit; and by artificially reducing natural populations every year, hunters actually stimulate breeding and cause higher birth rates. All the evidence indicates that hunting programs *cause* rather than cure or prevent wildlife degradation and overpopulation.

## H(a)unting Facts

- Hunting is permitted on 60 percent of U.S. wildlife refuges, and 45 percent of hunters do their killing on public lands. Such lands are supported by all taxpayers, and the U.S. Fish and Wildlife Service programs, which benefit hunters, receive as much as 90 percent of their funding from general tax revenues, not hunting fees.

- Wildlife "management" consists of herd manipulation designed to provide hunters with targets, not to spare deer from starvation, as hunters would like people to believe. It has resulted in a huge national deer population of 18 million. Hunters kill four million of these—mostly healthy males—and cripple another 600,000 annually.

- "Management" and hunters have virtually eliminated natural predators in most states; for example, trapping, poisoning, and shooting has reduced the wolf population to less than 2,000 in the lower 48 states.

- Today's crossbows pack 1,500 pounds of pressure. According to the Texas Wildlife Commission, bowhunters themselves report a 50 percent or higher wounding rate. For each deer killed, 21 arrows are shot. Shot placement is random, and it is hard to hit vital organs; experienced bowhunters injure *more* deer than novice bowhunters, who most often miss completely.

## THE SOLUTION

Hunted animals cannot defend themselves against hunters' high-powered weapons, so concerned citizens must become active on their behalf. Here are ways to protect wildlife and thwart hunters:

- Deny hunters land to hunt on. Encourage your neighbors, especially those who own large tracts such as farms and ranches, to post "No Hunting" signs every 100 yards. Explain to them that aggressive human hunters with their powerful weapons are far more dangerous than wild animals who invariably flee, even if surprised.
- People in nursing homes love animals too. Follow activist Janet Palomis's lead by signing them up for *free* senior-citizen hunting licenses. Each license saves lives a real hunter might have taken. For hunts that issue a limited number of permits, apply for permits yourself. The permits are usually awarded through a simple lottery system.
- Create an environment hostile to hunting. Spread deer repellent (available at feed and hardware stores), or hang little mesh bags of human hair (from a salon or barber shop) two or three feet above the ground along deer tracks, warning deer that humans have invaded their terrain. If hunters use dogs in your area, sprinkle a female dog's urine in heavily hunted areas or spray a solution of chopped garlic cloves soaked in water or diluted lemon juice on leaves and trails to throw dogs off the scent. Remove the food piles hunters sometimes leave as bait in hunting areas and scatter human hair or urine over the area.
- Go into the woods the day before hunting season begins, and loudly play a radio or recordings of wolf howls and walk with dogs on leashes. Such tactics are particularly important for scattering younger animals who have not yet known the traumatizing experience of being hunted.
- Some areas outlaw the hunting of animals who are "baited." Before one hunting season, activist Dorothy O'Brien turned herself in to state game authorities for feeding local ducks and geese, thereby making their slaughter illegal.

- Look for announcements of scheduled hunts in newspapers and magazines. Contact the sponsors or local authorities and ask that the hunt be canceled, both for human and other-than-human safety. Circulate petitions in neighboring areas and picket the entrance to the hunting grounds, or arrange a peaceful civil disobedience action against hunting violence.

- During hunts, assemble a group of people early in the morning and use airhorns and whistles to warn animals into hiding. Or play the national anthem on a bugle or tape and see if the hunters stand up!

- Develop strong anti-hunting sentiment in your community by writing letters to the editors of local newspapers, meeting with neighbors, and getting on talk shows. Post anti-hunting fliers in parks and other community areas. Let your neighbors know that federal law recognizes that wildlife "belongs" to *all* people, most of whom don't hunt.

- Encourage your municipality to pass an ordinance that bans, in the interest of public safety, the use of weapons within its limits. Lobby for laws that require hunters to carry written permission from landowners to hunt on private land. Ask your congressional representatives to introduce bills prohibiting hunting and trapping on national wildlife refuges and all public land.

- Ask your governor to appoint *non*hunters to state fish and game departments and wildlife committees. Support the **Committee to Abolish Sport Hunting**'s **(C.A.S.H.)** attempts to get nonhunters on decision-making "game boards" in New York State. Contact C.A.S.H. at Box 43, White Plains, NY 10605.

- If the pro-hunting course "Project Wild" is taught in your public schools, meet with teachers and school officials and ask them not to allow it. Its propaganda is not accurate, and by advocating slaughter, it teaches students *dis*respect for life and the environment.

- Go "hunt sabbing" (on a hunt sabotage), or support others who do, by sending a check to **The Fund for Animals,** 200 West 57th Street, New York, NY 10019.

- Educate yourself and others by reading and distributing books that tell the truth about hunting (see chapter 7, "Educate to Liberate"). Ask public and school libraries to carry them, or donate copies.

- Before you support a wildlife or conservation group, ask for its policy statement on hunting. The National Wildlife Federation, the National Audubon Society, the Sierra Club, the Wilderness Society, and the World Wildlife Fund do not oppose hunting.
- Make your voice count for free-roaming animals. Send PETA a large self-addressed, stamped envelope with a note requesting anti-hunting fliers to post and distribute.

# 27 GET POLITICAL

Ever occur to you why some of us can be this much concerned with animals' suffering? Because government is not. Why not? Animals don't vote.          —PAUL HARVEY

All progressive legislation has always had its genesis in the mind of one person. In the long run it is the cumulative effect that matters. One can do much. And one and one and one can move mountains.
          —JOAN WARD-HARRIS, *Creature Comforts*

## THE PROBLEM

Other-than-human beings do not have a Bill of Rights—and they certainly do not have senators and representatives. Elected officials usually respond to issues involving other-than-humans only when their human constituents compel them to do so. An essential part of any movement for social change is the effort to create new legislation, and since other-than-humans can't vote and can't lobby for themselves, we are responsible for making their concerns a political priority.

### A Bit of Background

The United States was the first country to enact animal protection legislation. In 1641, the Puritans included in their first legal code: "No man shall exercise any Tirrany or Crueltie towards any bruite Creature which are usually kept for man's use." However, America's record of animal mistreatment has caused most of us to forget this early legislative recognition of animal rights. Ironically, the U.S. has been one of the last Western countries to enact basic humane slaughter and laboratory animal welfare legislation—and only through hard-fought battles.

In 1955, Hubert Humphrey introduced the first humane slaughter bill ever presented to Congress—a bill the American Meat Institute called "premature" (eighty-two years after the enactment of Switzerland's law). The legislation faced strong opposition by powerful lobbies, but perseverance by Senator Humphrey, who despite suffering from a terrible bout with pneumonia left his sickbed to argue for its passage from the floor of the Senate, and groups like the Animal Welfare Institute eventually ensured passage of the bill (weakened only by a kosher exemption amendment) in 1958. It took effect in 1960. By law, "humane slaughter" (which many believe is a contradiction in terms) means either: (1) a method whereby the animal is rendered insensible to pain . . . before being [killed], or (2) a method in accordance with ritual requirements of the Jewish faith . . . whereby the animal suffers loss of consciousness by anemia of the brain [by] severance of the carotoid arteries with a sharp instrument.

The Laboratory Animal Welfare Act was signed into law in 1966. The culmination of six years of struggle against medical and pharmaceutical interests, it was the fifth federal statute passed in the U.S. designed to protect animals from abuse. Initially, it set care standards for dogs, cats, primates, rabbits, hamsters, and guinea pigs in animal dealers' premises and in laboratories prior to their experimental use. In 1970, Congress amended the act to require the use of anesthetics, analgesics, and tranquilizers during and after experiments, except when the experimenter could prove that the use of such drugs would defeat the purpose of the experiment. In 1976, amendments sponsored by Thomas Foley improved enforcement procedures, research institutions and government agencies were made a little more accountable, and amendments concerning transportation were added. In 1985, amendments sponsored by Bob Dole and George Brown required researchers to exercise dogs regularly, promote the "psychological well-being" of other-than-human primates, and increase cage sizes. The amended Animal Welfare Act is designed: (1) to ensure that animals intended for use in research facilities or for exhibition purposes or for use as companion animals are provided (*very*) minimum standards of care and treatment; (2) to provide minimal protections for animals during transportation in commerce; and (3) to protect the "owners" of animals from the theft of their animals by preventing the sale or use of animals who have been stolen. The act still does not protect birds, rats, and mice (the most common laboratory "tools"), farm animals, reptiles, or horses; the actual conduct of experiments still remains outside the provisions of the law; and compliance inspections are faulty and few and far between.

## WHAT YOU CAN DO

- Help political candidates who are sympathetic to animal issues get elected by joining their campaigns. Red Swift, a delegate to the convention that nominated Virginia governor Douglas Wilder, says, "Political success is like gardening. Nothing happens until the seed goes in the ground." Swift and activist Betty Lou LaJoy worked on Wilder's campaign, and Wilder became the nation's first major party statewide candidate ever to issue a statement on animal rights ("Doug Wilder Speaks Out on Animal Rights"). He said, in part: "Thousands of Virginians call for more humane treatment of animals, and I sympathize with them. . . . As Governor, I will closely study any legislation designed to extend this protection [of pound animals] to all areas of the state."

- Support animal protective legislation:

  • Introduced by Barbara Boxer (D-CA), the Consumer Products Safe Testing Act (H.R. 1676) would prohibit using the Lethal Dose 50 test for product safety, labeling, and transportation requirements, and would require federal agencies to review animal toxicity tests and to replace them when valid alternatives exist (many do!). (The LD-50 test is an out-dated acute toxicity test that determines the amount of a substance, eaten or otherwise internalized by "test" animals, that will kill 50 percent of a "test population." The test usually takes two-to-four weeks.)

  • H.R. 2345 (sponsored by Charlie Rose, D-NC) amends the Animal Welfare Act (AWA) to permit citizens to sue the United States Department of Agriculture to compel it to enforce the Animal Welfare Act.

• H.Con.Res. 5, a bill sponsored by Andrew Jacobs (D-IN), would mandate that federally funded schools provide students with meatless meal options.

• The **National Alliance for Animal Legislation,** P.O. Box 75116, Washington, DC 20013, (703) 684-0654, has information on pending legislation concerning animals who are hunted or trapped, marine mammals, wildlife and environment, farm animals, animals used in entertainment, regional refuges, and companion animals.

• Follow the example of activist Frank Branchini who, through **Maryland Law,** a group he founded, mass mails legislative action alerts, lobbies, and coordinates a statewide telephone tree to flood the switchboards of elected officials with support for animal protective legislation.

● Get acquainted with your elected officials. Find out who they are by calling the county board of elections or the League of Women Voters for a list of federal, state, county, and city officials. Get to know as many legislators as you can. Attend town meetings where legislators mingle with voters and where you can stand up and let them know you want them to learn about animal suffering and act to prevent it. Always thank them for taking the right position. Get to know the elected officials' aides, who are often more accessible, and who can provide you with timely "inside" information.

● When meeting personally with an elected official:

• Make an appointment well in advance.
• Dress conservatively and professionally.
• Be prompt and patient.
• Be friendly and positive.

● Don't forget to:

• Do your homework ahead of time.
• Learn about the legislator and her/his voting record.
• Compliment her/him on past accomplishments.

● Know your facts, provide one-page fact sheets and/or background information, make your points clearly and succinctly—and *rea-*

*sonably* (dispel the stereotype that animal advocates are emotional saps). Always thank the legislator for her/his time.

• Think creatively. Lisa Orr flew to Washington from Texas to present every member of Congress with a copy of John Robbins's *Diet for a New America*. She and her assistant talked with each legislator or aide, eliciting a positive response from virtually everyone. Ohio members of Protect Our Earth's Treasures (POET) countered the National Pork Producers Council's offer to Ohio legislators of a free ham-and-cheese lunch with that of a free, healthful, vegetarian sandwich lunch, which they delivered to legislators' offices along with information on the environmental and health consequences of eating meat.

• Capitalize on elected officials' understandable fear of bad press and penchant for photo (and other media-friendly) opportunities. The Tennessee Vegetarian Society blitzed the media when cattle-raiser Governor McWherter refused to proclaim October 1 Vegetarian Day and instead named October Beef Month. The activists got enough bad press for McWherter and good press for healthful eating to win an official Veggie Day in Tennessee.

• Write letters. When writing to an elected official, discuss only one issue in each letter, and keep it short (one page). *Legibly* handwritten letters are best—the more personal the letter appears, the more seriously it will be taken. Use personal or business stationery with a return address, and if you are a constituent, make that clear. Spell out all important details of the issue (don't assume the official knows *anything* about it), support your argument with facts, and state clearly and simply what you want her/him to do. Don't be vague.

• When writing U.S. representatives and senators, use the proper form for the address and salutation. Legislators are called "Honorable" on the envelope and as part of the inside address. The salutation for state or federal representatives is "Mr." or "Ms." The salutation for state or federal senators is "Senator." The address for a U.S. representative is: The Honorable _____ ; U.S. House of Representatives; Washington, DC 20515. The address for a U.S. senator is: The Honorable _____ ; U.S. Senate; Washington, DC 20510. The address for the president is: President Bush; 1600 Pennsylvania Avenue NW; Washington, DC 20516.

● *Sample postcard:*

Dear [legislator's name]:

I am writing to urge your support of H.R. 2596, the bill to
have the Silver Spring monkeys released to a sanctuary. These
animals have suffered greatly and deserve to live out their
remaining years in peace. Thank you.

Sincerely,
[Signature]
[Name, address]

● Contact groups that make animal protection legislation a top priority:

  • **National Alliance for Animal Legislation:** P.O. Box 75116,
  Washington, DC 20013; (703) 684-0654. Promotes pro-animal
  legislation, holds educational workshops, and issues action alerts
  and reports.
  • **Society for Animal Protective Legislation:** P.O. Box 3719,
  Georgetown Station, Washington, DC 20007; (202) 337-2334.
  Companion group to the Animal Welfare Institute; lobbies for
  federal animal protective legislation; issues action-alerts on critical
  pieces of legislation.
  • **Animal Political Action Committee (ANPAC):** P.O. Box 2706,
  Washington, DC 20077-9070. Helps elect federal legislators who
  are committed to acting in behalf of animals; publishes a voter's
  guide ($2) before congressional elections; and organizes volunteers
  to work on campaigns of supportive candidates.
  • **Animals' Lobby:** Capitol Plaza Building, 1025 Ninth Street,
  Suite 219, Sacramento, CA 95814; (916) 441-1562. Issues action
  alerts, legislative updates, and end-of-year updates on politicians'
  voting records.

# 28 INVEST IN COMPASSION

Whenever people say, 'We mustn't be sentimental,' you can take it they are about to do something cruel. And if they add, 'We must be realistic,' they mean they are going to make money out of it.

—**BRIGID BROPHY**

They used to say that knowledge is power. I used to think so, but I now know that they mean money.

—**LORD BYRON**, 1788–1824

## BACKGROUND

Until recently, the debate about the corporate use of animals existed almost entirely outside of the institutions responsible for using the animals. In 1985, it entered the annual meetings of three companies in the form of shareholder resolutions. Peter Lovenheim, then an attorney with the Humane Society of the United States, won an injunction that forced Iroquois Brands company to include an animal rights resolution in its proxy statement concerning the force-feeding of geese to make liver pâté—overruling the Security and Exchange Commission staff's position that the resolution did not pose a significant social issue.

Starting in 1987, PETA began using shareholder resolutions to gain official entrance to the annual meetings of nine major companies to protest their animal use, and in 1990, shareholder resolutions began to be used for animal issues other than testing. PETA submitted a resolution to American Express in 1990, seeking a ban on its fur sales, the ASPCA submitted challenges to factory farming to McDonald's and Pepsico, and several groups have proposed resolutions to U.S. Surgical in 1989 and 1990 on the company's use of dogs to teach sales people how to operate surgical staple guns.

## LEVER(AGE) OF CHANGE

A recent report by the Investor Responsibility Research Center found that six of the nine companies targeted by animal rights organizations' "Corporate Responsibility" projects had dramatically reduced the numbers of animals they used by an average of 42 percent between 1986 and 1988. Some stockbrokers, investment companies, and security analysts, like Wedbush Morgan, are also acting to steer investors away from companies exploiting animals, the most obvious being corporations and industries directly involved in the meat and dairy business, cosmetics companies that still test on animals, and the fur trade.

- If you are a broker or investment banker, follow the lead of vegetarian commodities broker Susan Sjo, who refuses to trade beef and pork futures and tells her clients why.
- If you own stock, use it as leverage to change corporate practices. Join PETA's Corporate Responsibility Project, or a similar plan, or draft your own resolution. For example, lend your name to an animal protection shareholder proposal: if you have owned $1000 worth of stock in a company for one year or longer, you are eligible to sign onto existing shareholder proposals as a co-proponent. This would involve no work other than furnishing proof of ownership. Typical proposals ask companies to disclose detailed and closely guarded information to shareholders regarding their use of animals. Other proposals ask for an outright ban on an exploitative practice.
- *Leave Home Without It.* Your choice of credit card can send a message, too. If you are a cardholder and do not own stock in American Express, but feel strongly invested in getting the company to stop fur sales, cut your card in two and send the pieces to PETA. Then write the president of **American Express,** Louis V. Gerstner, Jr. (American Express, Amex Tower, 200 Vesey Street, New York, NY 10285-5120), telling him that you will

resume your membership only when the company makes a commitment to furbearing animals and caring (ex)cardholders.

- Take out an account with **Working Assets Funding Service,** San Francisco, CA, 1-800-522-7759 (8:30–5:30 Monday to Friday Pacific time), which donates a certain percentage of its proceeds to various nonprofits, such as Greenpeace. They issue donation-linked credit cards, and long-distance phone and travel services. Write them and nominate your favorite animal protection organizations as recipients.

- Use message checks. Most people write about three hundred checks a year, and each check is seen by merchants, clerks, tellers, and others. Every time you order a supply of message checks, your chosen charity makes about a dollar. For example, you can now speak out against animal testing with every check you write by ordering PETA Message! Checks. A number of organizations offer message checks—some with beautiful animal and nature pictures on them.

- Buy and give stock that supports ethical practices, choosing companies such as the Body Shop, Paul Mitchell Systems, and Aveda. To invest in companies that do not test on animals, consult with your stockbroker. PETA's Caring Consumer Campaign can advise if necessary.


## RESOURCE

- Copies of *Animal Testing and Consumer Products,* which examines the perspectives of companies, regulators, and activists in the debate over animal testing, are available for $25 each, prepaid, from the **Investor Responsibility Research Center,** 1755 Massachusetts Avenue NW, Suite 600, Washington, DC 20036; (202) 234-7500.

# 29 CORPORATE CRUELTY: FIVE AT A TIME

The citizens of the United States must effectively control the mighty commercial forces which they have themselves called into being.
—FRANKLIN DELANO ROOSEVELT

I definitely think large corporations are capable of doing good, but many of them are locked into old habits. Corporations are just like people: they often need to be jolted out of comfortable practices. That's what we're doing with cosmetics companies that test their products on animals—increasing their discomfort level.
—SUSAN RICH, in Phil Maggitti's "Susan Rich: Compassion Begins in the Home," *The Animals' Agenda,* May 1990

What L'Oréal does to animals makes me sick.
—MTV's JULIE BROWN

## THE PROBLEM

We were hard-pressed to pick the worst five—just five—corporations to reprimand for their laboratory treatment of animals. But, in the interest of space and convenience, we did limit our list to a chosen few and provide for you here the names, addresses, and phone numbers of five organizations considered currently in the winners' circle when it comes to deserving some focused public heat. More and more people are calling upon them and businesses like them to develop a conscience. In the cosmetics industry, that means acknowledging that other-than-humans are not ours to experiment on, and then seeking and using better ways to test products. These five industry giants are in a position to set the trend.

## THE SOLUTION

Petition, write, call, boycott, and return products (most companies have unconditional, money-back guarantees) to the following:

- **L'Oréal,** Guy Peyrelongue, president of Cosmair (U.S. division of L'Oréal and Lancôme), 575 Fifth Avenue, New York, NY 10017; 1-800-631-7358. Also, Lindsay Owen-Jones, president of L'Oréal, 41 Rue Martre, 92117 Clichy, France:

  • *Products:* L'Oréal make-up and hair-care products, Studio Line, Performing Preference hair dyes, Paloma Picasso Perfumes, Ambre Solaire suntan lotion; also, Lancôme cosmetics (shares L'Oréal's parent company in the U.S., Cosmair).
  • People are learning that the world's most profitable cosmetics company is also one of the cruelest. To date, L'Oréal won't agree to stop poisoning and killing animals, even though non-animal tests are now in use by more than three hundred "cruelty-free" companies.
  • L'Oréal claims only 5 percent of its products are tested on animals. Given that other major companies, such as Avon, Estée Lauder, and Revlon have given up animal tests altogether, it should not be so difficult for L'Oréal to follow suit.
  • L'Oréal executive vice president James Nixon, who is in a position to change his company's cosmetics testing practices, has said, "I'm not a scientist, but the tests sound crazy to me." Still, he has resisted taking a stand against the tests.
  • L'Oréal has tried to console people concerned about their animal testing by telling them they test "only" on rats and mice—thereby minimizing the importance of animals known to be as sentient as any others.

• One of L'Oréal's sunscreen product tests involved frying live hairless mice wrapped in foil.

● **Gillette Company,** Prudential Tower Building, Boston, MA 02199 (CEO: Colman Mockler); (617) 421-7000:

• *Products:* In addition to its razors and blades (including the Sensor razor, which the company recently introduced with a $175 million fanfare), Gillette makes such toiletries and cosmetics as Right Guard deodorant, Foamy brand shaving cream, Toni Home Perms, and Aapri and Jafra cosmetics. The company also sells Liquid Paper correction fluid and Paper Mate and Flair pens.
• When Gillette's testing practices were first exposed in 1985, so many customers returned their products that Gillette has since changed its refund policy and canceled its toll-free telephone number. To receive a refund, complainants to Gillette must currently state, "I find the performance of these Gillette products to be unsatisfactory, and I am demanding a full refund." (Be sure to tell them that you have found a wonderful *cruelty-free* brand to use in their product's place.) Be warned that Gillette will *not* now refund products to people complaining about its testing on other-than-human beings. Still, you might try ending your refund request letter with, "P.S. I also think you should *stop* testing your products on animals, and I will not try your products again until you do so." Or send your Gillette products to the **New England Anti-Vivisection Society (NEAVS),** 333 Washington Street, Suite 850, Boston, MA 02108-5100. They will use them in their periodic "product dumps" on Gillette's front door.
• Environmental organizations and anti-apartheid groups have joined animal rights organizations in an international boycott of Gillette, in protest of the company's "irresponsible social practices." At an April 1990 protest at Gillette's world headquarters in Boston, demonstrators presented the company with the "Green Genie Bad Neighbor Award," reprimanding Gillette's continued air and water pollution, production of petroleum-based plastic materials, use of animals in product testing, and refusal to divest holdings in South Africa.

● **Johnson & Johnson,** One Johnson & Johnson Plaza, New Brunswick, NJ 08933 (CEO: Ralph Larsen); 1-800-526-3967:

• *Products:* Baby shampoo, Sundown sunscreen, Shower-to-Shower Body Powder, and Stayfree and Carefree feminine hygiene products.

• J&J reported in spring 1989 that laboratory animal use for nonmedical consumer products has dropped 80 percent since 1983, "including animals used in eye and skin irritation studies," but it has not substantiated this figure.

• One of J&J's best-known products is its "no more tears" baby shampoo. But really, no amount of animal testing can make it desirable to put *any* shampoo in the eye. Mothers today recall experiencing—and seeing their own children now experience—a *large* amount of tears and pain when accidentally getting Johnson's Baby Shampoo in the eyes.

● **Cheesebrough-Ponds, Inc.,** 33 Benedict Place, Greenwich, CT 06830 (CEO: Richard Finn); 1-800-243-5804 or (203) 661-2000:

• *Products:* Cutex nail polish remover; Pond's beauty creams, lotions, and bars; Rave hair-care products; Vaseline products; Aim; Close-Up; Pepsodent; Signal; Impulse; Prince Matchabelli division (Aziza cosmetics, Erno Laszlo skin care); and a recently acquired Fabergé division (which, to date, will not sign a Statement of Assurance that it does not test on animals).

• As companies such as Cheesebrough-Ponds are trying to assure customers that they are taking measures to reduce and eliminate the use of animals in product testing, the actual amount of testing is on the rise. According to an article in the *Toronto Star* ("Cosmetics firms up research spending"): "The beauty industry, founded on image and marketing, is turning more and more to science to give sales a boost," wrote Elizabeth Collier. It is in the name of science that so many animal tests are done—"new" and "improved" products almost invariably mean more animal tests.

● **Clairol, Inc.** (subsidiary of **Bristol-Myers Squibb**), 345 Park Avenue, New York, NY 10154 (CEO: Richard L. Gelb); 1-800-223-5800 or (212) 546-5000:

• *Products:* Final Net hair spray, Sea Breeze, Condition hair products, and the following hair dyes: Nice 'n' Easy, Miss Clairol, Loving Care, and Ultress.

• Clairol's own materials and data demonstrate that safety is clearly not the reason it uses the Draize eye-irritancy test; if it were, products that were Draize-tested and appeared to be unsafe would not be marketed. Instead, information Clairol itself has released reveals that many of the products it markets are acknowledged eye irritants, and some can cause permanent eye damage. (Clairol's notice regarding its permanent hair colors reads: "CAUTION. Eye irritants . . . the mixture may cause severe irritation and possible permanent eye injury.")

• Testing cosmetics on other-than-human beings is not necessary for caution labeling (a general-purpose label should be mandatory on all potentially harmful products). Neither is it contributing to knowledge about how to treat eye injuries—animals are not treated but simply killed after a test or 'recycled' into more tests.

• Clairol's Dr. John Corbitt has claimed that the Dermal Skin Test causes no more discomfort to animals than a man feels when shaving.

• Erwin Whitman, M.D., Bristol-Myers' vice president of medical affairs, has said, "If we only look at it from the point of view of efficiency and economy, we are much better off doing anything we do *in vitro* (non-animal) than in animals because it's cheaper, it's quicker, more reliable, there's less variation—everything about it is better." Clairol would do well to follow his advice.

**Note:** Boycotts are most effective when enacted *en masse!* Circulate a petition in your neighborhood, office and/or school. Collect products and return them in a large package addressed to the company's CEO or chairperson. Be sure to let the company know what and why you are boycotting.

## RESOURCES

• For a free page of "*Warning:* Cruelly Tested on Animals" stickers, send a self-addressed, stamped envelope to **PETA.**

• Write to **PETA** for a current and comprehensive address list of companies testing their products on animals.

# 30 MIND YOUR "BEES" AND "SHREWS"

Dismembering animals begins with dismembering language.
—Columnist COLMAN MCCARTHY

The man who is described as behaving 'like a beast' would often in his behavior be a disgrace to any known animal.
—ERNEST BELL

## THE PROBLEM

"Words, words, words," mused Shakespeare. No one can dispute their importance, and yet, we use them with an alarming lack of care.

Best-selling author and self-described "curmudgeon" Cleveland Amory points out that we often insult each other by calling each other animal names such as "pig," "swine," "weasel," "skunk," "baboon," or "jackass." We berate each other by using animal similes such as "mean as a snake," "stubborn as a mule," "crazy as a loon," and "silly as a goose." One person ridicules another with terms like "chicken," "bull-headed," or "dumb bunny;" and a questionable situation is "fishy." Derogatory words for *women* include "dog," "cow," "shrew," "vixen," and "bitch." Amory notes that one dictionary definition for *animal* is "a bestial person."

Unthinkingly, we develop callousness and indifference to animals by using language that is euphemistic, inaccurate, and deceptive. We label the flesh cut from animal corpses as "meat," "veal," "pork," "beef," or "poultry." The Department of Agriculture refers to cows, pigs, and

113

chickens as "grain-consuming animal units." As author Carol Adams writes, we have "institutionalized the oppression of animals on at least two levels: in formal structures such as slaughterhouses, meat markets, zoos, laboratories, and circuses, and through our language."

## THE SOLUTION

Liberate your language. Colman McCarthy writes: "Language shapes attitudes and attitudes shape behavior." As our society attempts to cleanse itself of racist and sexist language, so, too, must we become aware and get rid of speciesist language—adopting a vocabulary that is accurate and dignifying to other-than-human beings. The Blacker Group, a grass-roots group in the northeast, offers the following tips to help us choose our words carefully:

- Refer to all individuals with gender as "he" or "she," and never "it." ("It" refers only to inanimate objects.) Likewise, other-than-humans are "living *beings*" rather than "living *things*," and we should refer to them with the relative pronoun "who" rather than "which."
- Use "companion" in lieu of "pet"; and "guardian," "protector," or "friend" in place of "owner" and "master."
- Use honest and accurate language when referring to suffering and death. The terms "put to sleep," "sacrifice," and "harvest" are euphemisms for "kill"—or "murder" (unless the act is truly *euthanasia,* which Webster's dictionary describes as "the act or practice of killing for reasons of mercy").

# 31

# FIRST AID: BE PREPARED FOR ANIMAL EMERGENCIES

All the arguments to prove man's superiority cannot shatter this hard fact: in suffering the animals are our equals.

—**PETER SINGER,** *Animal Liberation*

To help life reach full development, the good [person] is a friend of all living things.

—**ALBERT SCHWEITZER,** *The Thought of Albert Schweitzer*

There is no doubt that much of what we know of medicine comes . . . from the birds and animals that we have watched.

—**M. F. K. FISHER,** *A Cordiall Water: A Garland of Odd and Old Receipts to Assuage the Ills of Man & Beast*

We have long known and used much that the birds and beasts have taught us. . . .

Animals go without any mystical query to the water or mud or herb that will help them, and as far as we can tell they do not question their going, nor pray to be led, nor offer their thanks when they are better. Neither do they need our aid, except of course when we have caged and domesticated them past their own help. But we need them and learn ceaselessly from them.

—**M. F. K. FISHER,** Ibid

## THE PROBLEM

Few humans get through life illness and accident free. The same is true, of course, for other-than-human beings. Just in case someone needs your help, it's a good idea to know some basic emergency-response techniques and what to watch for.

## THE SOLUTION

- In case of emergency, seek veterinary help right away. Describe symptoms or injuries clearly, and take careful note of instructions. Generally, keep the victim quiet and still; in the case of traffic accidents, move victims carefully and gently out of danger, and then follow these procedures: When waiting for a veterinarian, the general principle is to stem any bleeding (without cutting off circulation!) and keep air passages clear of obstructions while disturbing the animal as little as possible. If you need to carry an injured dog, make a stretcher out of a blanket, board, coat, or sack; put it on the ground and gradually slide it under him/her. Keep the stretcher taut. Stem bleeding with a clean handkerchief, piece of sheet, or any cloth by making a pad and securing it to the wound, then elevate the injured body part.
- Always carry emergency numbers of veterinarians in your wallet and keep them stuck to the telephone at home.
- An injured animal, however familiar, may snap or bite out of fear and pain. A bandage or belt can be used as a makeshift muzzle, looped around the snout a couple of times and then tied behind the head. Make sure the animal can breathe easily (watch out for heaving sides, a sign of breathing difficulty) and isn't vomiting or s/he may choke. Release the muzzle as soon as you can.
- Shock is a basic problem with any form of trauma; keep animals as quiet and warm as possible. If possible, put one person strictly in charge of monitoring the animal.
- Carry Bach Flower Rescue Remedy in case of emergency (available from **InterNatural,** P.O. Box 580, Shaker Street, S. Sutton, NH 03273; (603) 927-4776; and **Ellon (Bach USA) Inc.,** P.O. Box

320, Woodmere, NY 11598; (516) 593-2206. A few drops on the lips can calm shock, and the remedy is effective for both humans and other-than-humans.

- Beware that human medicines may not be suitable for other-than-humans, and some can have disastrous results—aspirin, for example, can be fatal to cats. The therapeutic needs of other-than-human beings can also be quite different from ours, due to differences in physiology. Since rats and horses cannot vomit, giving them something to induce vomiting may make the situation worse. Always check with a veterinarian first.

- The following symptoms, in any combination, should always be taken very seriously:

  - Bleeding from any orifice: nose, mouth, ears, rectum, sex organs
  - Any problems with eyes: watering or half-closed, third eyelid exposed
  - Straining to urinate or repeated trips to the litterbox
  - Bloating or collapse after eating, exercise, or rapid intake of water
  - Unusually lethargic or agitated behavior
  - Drinking lots of water
  - Fur standing on end
  - Loss of appetite
  - Continuous vomiting
  - Dragging or holding limbs
  - Sudden weight loss
  - Diarrhea
  - Coughing
  - Lumps

- Advice for particular problems:

  - *Choking.* Try to look in the mouth, and check the tongue, roof of the mouth, teeth, and gums. Holding the tongue with a handkerchief will make looking down the throat easier. If you see any objects stuck (i.e., sticks, bones, small balls) try very gently to get them out, but be careful; most will have to be removed by the veterinarian under anesthesia. If you cannot reach the object, hold your companion upside down and shake her. A sharp blow on the back of the neck or between the shoulders will sometimes dislodge a blunt object from the throat. Get to a veterinarian *ASAP*. As a last resort, use a modified Heimlich maneuver. Place your hands on either side of your companion's rib cage, then give her a very quick, firm squeeze to rapidly compress the lungs. If administered incorrectly, it can cause additional injuries, so ask your veterinarian to demonstrate the proper method to use for your companion animal.

• *When your companion animal stops breathing.* Artificial respiration and cardiopulmonary resuscitation (CPR) may be required if your friend stops breathing. To give artificial resuscitation, clear a cat's or dog's mouth of any foreign matter, and then close it. Cover her nostrils with a clean, thin cloth or gauze. Exhale directly into the nostrils 12-to-15 breaths per minute. If the heart is not beating, it may be necessary to concurrently conduct CPR. Have someone transport you and your companion animal to the veterinarian's office while you are performing CPR. Ask your veterinarian to demonstrate the proper procedure for your companion animal.

• *Drowning.* Swing a small animal gently upside down by the hind legs to evacuate the water inside and apply mouth-to-mouth resuscitation, if necessary.

• *(Suspected) Poisoning.* Since some animals are physiologically unable to vomit, get clear instructions for an antidote from a veterinarian familiar with the species. Call an animal poison hotline number for immediate help. The **Illinois Animal Poison Information Center,** 1-800-548-2423, provides around-the-clock advice, and charges $25 per call with a VISA or Mastercard or $30 otherwise (a small price to pay to save a friend's life!). The **Georgia Animal Poison Information Center,** (404) 542-6751, can also give advice, but is open only from nine to five, Monday through Friday.

• *Heat prostration.* First get the animal out of the sun and heat. Then the animal should be quickly hosed down, placed in a tub of cool water, or wrapped in wet rags until the body temperature is lowered. Finally, treat for shock and/or have a veterinarian administer intravenous fluids, if necessary.

## RESOURCES

- *First Aid for Pets,* Robert W. Kirk, D.V.M. (New York: Dutton, 1978).
- *Emergency Care for Cats and Dogs,* Craton Burkholder, D.V.M. (New York: Michael Kesend Publishing, 1987).
- *The Complete Book of Cat Health* and *The Complete Book of Dog Health,* by William J. Kay, D.V.M., with Elizabeth Randolph (New York: MacMillan, 1985).

# 32 | IMPROVING A DOG'S LIFE

My little old dog;
A heart-beat at my feet.
>—**EDITH WHARTON,** from "A Lyrical Epigram"
>(as quoted in *The Extended Circle,* by Jon Wynne-Tyson)

How would you like to live in a cage/ that way just about ten feet square/ with no toys to play with and nothing to do—/ just you and a bed and a chair? . . . You'd get mad and scream and/ throw things around;/ you'd kick and you'd paint on the wall,/ and your owners would/ scold you,/ and say to themselves,/ "He isn't a nice pet at all!"
>—**BEVERLY ARMSTRONG,** "Where the Wild Things
>Shouldn't Be," *The Animals' Voice,* April 1989

Pets, like kings' favourites, are usually the recipients of an abundance of sentimental affection but of little real kindness; so much easier is it to give temporary caresses than substantial justice.
>—**HENRY S. SALT,** *Animals' Rights*

**ONLY HER FELINE FRIEND WOULD KNOW:** According to *Harper's* "Index," 57 percent of cat "owners" say they confide in their cats about important matters.

## THE PROBLEM

Food, shelter, and water do not a life make—at least not a great life. All warm beings need love, affection, interesting activities, and the knowledge that they are *important* to someone. Too many animals merely exist in human homes, loved in the back of busy people's minds, but benignly neglected.

## THE SOLUTION

Give your other-than-human companion a gift (or two or three) that will make her/him happier:

- *Quality time.* To turn off that television and resolve to walk and play daily with your faithful companion animal is the best present of all. For birds, rabbits, hamsters, and other caged-for-safety companions, daily open-door time with you, in an accident-proof room, is a must.
- *Interspecies communication.* Does your "interaction" with your dog consist only of reprimands? Is your side of the "conversation" limited to commands, such as "sit," "stay," "down," "shut up," and "stop it"? According to PETA librarian Karen Porreca, animals try to communicate with us all the time. She writes:

> It's important to pay attention to your dog's body language—his or her primary means of getting through to you. A stare, a wag of the tail, a paw on your knee, a whimper—ignoring these "remarks" is tantamount to ignoring your friend's "hello" or "I'm in need of something." Even if you do nothing more than wink or make a reassuring clucking sound or say, "I see you," at least you've acknowledged your dog's communication.
>
> Dogs also have a wide range of vocal expressions. In addition to whines, whimpers and growls, they have quite a variety of different barks. By paying close attention you will quickly learn the difference between barks that mean "I'm so happy to see you" and "There's

a cat outside the window'' and ''I'm having fun playing'' and ''There's a strange human at the door.'' Understanding your dog's message gives you the opportunity to respond appropriately.

- *A room with a view.* A cat or dog window perch or ramp to relieve the boredom of wall watching.
- *A dog/cat door* (into a fenced yard, of course). For relief of a different, more urgent sort—no one expects *human* beings to keep their legs crossed for 8 to 10 hours a day! If cats can come and go unattended, be sure to safeguard Tiddles by adding a 45-degree interior angle to the top of your fencing. Cats and cars don't mix.
- *A permanent house guest.* Dogs are pack animals, so don't let your companion's world consist of you, and only you. After all, you're not always home and can never *fully* understand subtle canine lingo and needs. A companion from the local pound can make a world of difference.
- *Something to chew on.* Tennis balls and rubber, rope or nylon (*not* rawhide) chew toys.
- *A foam pad to rest and sleep on.* This will keep dogs and cats out of drafts and provide relief from arthritis and protection for joints, especially older ones.
- *A kiddie swimming pool.* Cool relief for dogs in the summer. (If other small mammals inhabit your yard, keep a stone or brick in the pool at the edge to make sure any animals that fall in can also climb out.)
- *Your patience (is a virtue).* Never scold your dog for not understanding you. Writes PETA's Porreca:

> It's important to actively teach your dogs the things you want them to understand. Imagine how you would feel if someone who had some kind of ''power'' over you (such as your boss or your parents, when you were little) told you to do something, using words that you couldn't understand, and then punished or scolded you when you didn't do it. Or suppose you were trying to learn a foreign language and the teacher kept changing the meanings of the words, so that it was impossible for you to learn them. This is what we do to our companion dogs when we expect them to understand English without ever having been taught any. It's unfair to them and very distressing.

- *Cat Dancer*. A simple, wire toy that cats flip over. Available from **Action Cat Toys Mail Shop,** 111 E. Canal Street, Neenah, WI 54956, and from many pet stores, for about $3.
- *Dandy Dog Life Preserver*. Provides security for the boating dog in your life. Available in six different sizes from **Pedigrees,** 15 Turner Drive, Spencerport, NY 14559-0110; (716) 352-1232. Prices start around $25.
- *An expandable leash*. Its self-adjusting, controllable length reduces pulling and tugging. Available at many pet supply stores and directly from **Flexi USA, Inc.,** 3695-G, N. 126th Street, Brookfield, WI 53005; (414) 783-5767.

## RECREATIONAL READING

- *Mother Knows Best: the Natural Way to Train Your Dog,* by Carol Lea Benjamin, available from Howell Book House, Inc., 230 Park Ave., New York, NY 10169.
- *Communicating with Your Dog: A Humane Approach to Dog Training,* by Ted Baer, available from Barron's Educational Series, Inc., 250 Wireless Boulevard, Hauppage, NY 11788.

# 33
# "RATS!" (...AND OTHER RODENTS)

None of our fellow mortals is safe who eats what we eat, who in any way interferes with our pleasures, or who may be used for work or food, clothing or ornament, or mere cruel, sportish amusement. Fortunately many are too small to be seen, and therefore enjoy life beyond our reach. And . . . it is a great comfort to learn that vast multitudes of creatures, great and small and infinite in number, lived and had a good time . . . before man [existed].

—**JOHN MUIR**, "Stickeen: An Adventure with a Dog and a Glacier"

It is much easier to arouse sympathy for dogs, cats and primates . . . but, ultimately it may be the lowly rat who truly tests if humanity is worthy of extending its presence to new realms. There may be no greater example of the withholding of compassion to a whole species than our present treatment of the domesticated rat.

—**DANIEL VAN ARSDALE** (courtesy Buddhists Concerned for Animals)

## THE PROBLEM

Finding rodent droppings, hearing the patter of little feet, and noticing chew marks in your library books can pose a dilemma for people who care about animals. Most find it untenable to put up with indoor rodents but feel equally strongly that "exterminating" them is out of the question. Traditional methods of rodent control–like poisons and anticoagulants inflict enormous suffering on these little beings, who are certainly as capable of suffering as any other animal and who are only trying to survive. Fortunately, alternatives exist!

**Rat Fact:** Number of reported cases of humans bitten by rats in New York City in 1985: 311. Number reported bitten by other people: 1,519 (*Harper's* "Index").

## THE SOLUTION

While we may not want to sign over our lease to the local mice and rats, we must discourage their tenancy or effect their relocation in as humane and civilized a manner as possible. Some guidelines:

- *Never* use a glue trap. Rodents caught in glue traps can struggle for days before they are found and are frequently thrown into the trash alive. Trapped animals, struggling to free themselves, often pull out their own hair and sometimes bite off their own legs. The glue causes their eyes to become badly irritated and swollen, and those whose faces get stuck in it slowly suffocate. All trapped animals experience stress, trauma, and dehydration.
- Rodent infestation is largely *preventable* by maintaining clean, sanitary conditions. Dry up the food supply and your visiting rat family will have to go out to eat. Do not leave human, dog, or cat food lying around. Sweep and wipe up crumbs, and put leftovers away. Store dry goods such as rice, birdseed, crackers, breakfast cereals, and flour in sealed containers made of metal, glass, or ceramic with tight-fitting lids rather than in paper or plastic bags. Keep fruits and vegetables in the refrigerator.
- Plug holes or cracks, where mice or rats might reenter, with mesh or tar paper, then plaster or caulking.
- Use a humane, nonlethal trap. Available from many humane societies and hardware stores, these traps typically consist of a plastic or metal box with a spring-release trap door that shuts once the rodent enters in search of food. The trap can then be taken outdoors where s/he can be released unharmed. Beware of tube traps without air vents, which can cause the frightened animal to suffocate. A good reusable, humane mousetrap is available for $10 from **Sea-**

**bright,** Dept. 2, 4026 Harlan Street, Emeryville, CA 94608. Check your trap 16 billion times a day! (Wild animals in traps experience extreme distress and can even injure themselves attempting to get free.)

- If your local stores sell glue traps and/or poison for rats and mice, please complain in person to the manager, suggesting alternatives. A couple in Allentown, Pennsylvania, successfully protested and boycotted their local True Value store. They are now leading the effort to get the entire franchise to stop carrying glue traps. Please support them by writing to Mr. Daniel Cotter, president, **True Value,** Cotter and Company, 2740 Clybourne Avenue, Chicago, IL 60614.

# 34 NO SKIN OFF THEIR BACKS

To my mind the life of the lamb is no less precious than that of a human being. I should be unwilling to take the life of the lamb for the sake of the human body. I hold that, the more helpless a creature, the more entitled it is to protection by man from the cruelty of man.
—MOHANDAS K. GANDHI,
*An Autobiography: The Story of My Experiments*

A May 1990 poll in *Parents Magazine* (vol. 65, no. 5, p. 33) indicated that 69 percent of people polled considered themselves against killing animals for leather—46 percent of whom said it should be illegal.

## THE PROBLEM

In Australia, it's not the bloody fur trade they have to combat, it's the wool industry; yet, in this country we are oblivious to the massive suffering of sheep on foreign mega-farms. Most of us are equally unaware of the suffering stitched into each silk blouse, down pillow, and pair of leather shoes derived from slaughterhouse activity on our own turf. The garment industry has changed dramatically over the years: animal-derived clothing has meant increased cruelties due to factory-farming practices, while natural fiber and synthetics have become increasingly "cool." Nowadays, given a heightened awareness and an eye for "compassionate clothing," no one has to dress like a Neanderthal cave-dweller to look great and feel comfortable.

## Leather Logic

- Leather, like fur, of course, is the skin of once-living animals, and really, who wants to wear that? Because leather is a slaughterhouse by-product, buying and wearing it directly supports the factory-farming industry and its systematic, mass animal exploitation. As leathermaking has become a multibillion dollar industry, many of the largest meat producers also run their own leather tanneries now.

- When a 1000-pound steer is slaughtered, 432 pounds of retail beef are produced, the rest of the carcass going to the manufacture of by-products. Skin accounts for 50 percent of the total by-product value of cattle. When dairy cows' production declines, their skin is also made into leather; and the hides of their offspring, veal calves, are made into high-priced calfskin.

- According to the Tanners' Council of America's *U.S. Leather Industry Statistics,* every year, approximately 230 million cattle, 350 million sheep, 175 million goats, and 700 million pigs are slaughtered worldwide for their flesh and skin.

- The principal driving force behind the destruction of tropical rain forests is the U.S. fast-food hamburger habit; and the skin of the Latin American cattle provides North Americans with cheap duds—the adornment equivalent of a Big Mac.

- Most of the leather produced and sold in the U.S. is made from skins of cattle and calves, but leather is also made from the hides of horses, sheep, lambs, goats, kids, and pigs slaughtered for meat. Myriad other species around the world are hunted and killed specifically for their skins, including zebras, buffaloes, deer, kangaroos, elephants, tigers, ostriches, eels, sharks, whales, seals, frogs, crocodiles, mules, and lizards. Up to one-third of "exotic" leathers come from endangered, illegally poached animals.

- All animal-skin products imply suffering.

  - Reptiles such as alligators and snakes are usually conscious when skinned to make shoes, handbags, and belts because no one can be bothered or wants to incur the extra expense involved in stunning them. Cold-blooded reptiles also take far longer to die than do mammals—hours, sometimes days.

• Young Karakul goats are boiled alive by shepherds to produce "kid" gloves because that tenderizes the skin.

• Wildlife in rivers and streams are killed by toxic chemicals dumped by the leather-tanning industry. There are also human health consequences: the Centers for Disease Control found that the incidence of leukemia among residents in an area surrounding one tannery in Kentucky was five times the national average.


## What's Wrong with Wool?

● Wool is the sheared coat of sheep. Breeders have created sheep called Merinos, who are extremely wrinkly (more wrinkles mean more wool). This unnatural overload of wool causes many sheep to die of heat exhaustion in the summer, as well as of exposure to cold and damp after late shearing (a closely shorn sheep is more sensitive to cold than even a naked human, since a sheep's normal body temperature is much higher than ours). In Australia (where 80 percent of all wool used in clothing originates, and where about 158 million sheep are raised for wool and then slaughtered every year), each year approximately 6.3 million sheep die on the farm, and up to 10 percent of all sheep die on their way to slaughterhouses in the Middle East—largely from exposure.

● One of the worst and most painful wool industry practices is *mulesing:* slicing off large sections of a lamb's backside (skin, not wool) with shears—and *without* anesthesia. Farmers employ this practice because the bloody wound, when and *if* it heals three-to-five painful weeks later, will pull the skin tight and prevent moisture and urine from collecting in the (artificially wrinkly) Merino sheep's skin, which otherwise is a haven for blowflies and their eggs.

● Sheep are violently pinned down and often get cut from the rough shearing that is inevitable when speed means money. Farmers use a hot tar compound to seal bleeding wounds, which are especially prevalent on farms where computer-controlled shearing machinery holds the sheep's faces in a clamp, and a sensor directs a shearing comb that can fail to circumvent teats and other protrusions.

● Lambs endure ear-punching, tail-docking (having their tails cut off) and castration; and aging sheep are subjected to *tooth-grinding,* a procedure in which unanesthetized sheep are restrained and have their teeth cut down to the gums, exposing the sensitive pulp cavities inside.

- Millions of sheep are exported live to the Middle East each year by ship. Packed tightly, they travel great distances, and for weeks are forced to stand in (and eat food tainted by) urine and feces. Those who arrive alive are slaughtered by having their throats slit. (According to one witness, "The sheep would wave their heads in obvious confusion, trying to stand up and call out as the blood gushed from their throats.")

## Down Is Out

- Down is the insulating feathers of ducks and geese. Most down in pillows, parkas, and comforters comes from birds who have endured a life of preparation for the slaughterhouse (a customer service agent of The Company Store in Wisconsin described the source of the down and feathers in their products as "the natural by-product of the European food industry"). The rest derives from geese raised for down; and anyone who has plucked her/his eyebrows can (only begin to) imagine how painful it is for these animals to have all their feathers pulled from their necks and breasts—not just once, but four or five times during their short lives.

## So Is Silk!

Silk comes from the shiny fiber that silkworms make to form their cocoons. Many people think of it as "natural," not realizing that farmers boil or steam the silkworms alive in their cocoons by the thousands. (The International Silk Association states in its brochure "What Is Silk?" that "it is necessary to destroy the worm inside the cocoon if the silk is to be reeled. This is done by stifling it with heat.") It is well established that silkworms can feel pain.

## WHAT YOU CAN DO

- Purchase only non-leather shoes, clothing, and accessories (including watchbands, soccer balls, upholstery, belts, etc.). Alternatives include cotton, linen, rayon, canvas, nylon, ramie, rubber, and vinyl, whose advantages include affordability and ease of cleaning. Today there are many comfortable, well-made, and fashionable non-leather alternatives, such as satin dress shoes, synthetic running shoes, and canvas recreation shoes. Among other companies, Nike, Asics, New Balance, Naturalizer, Kenneth Cole, Hush Puppies, Thom McAn, Payless, Banana Republic, L. L. Bean, Talbot's, Carroll Reed, and Appleseed's have attractive, quality, non-leather shoes. Look closely at your mail-order catalogues and, when out shopping, don't be afraid to ask salespeople for help finding non-leather footwear. Some mail-order catalogues *specializing* in non-leather shoes, belts, wallets, and accessories include:

  - **Aesop Unlimited,** 55 Fenno Street, P.O. Box 315, Cambridge, MA 02140
  - **Life Stride/Brown Shoe Company,** P.O. Box 354, Saint Louis, MO 63166
  - **The Compassionate Consumer,** P.O. Box 27, Jericho, NY 11753
  - **Old Pueblo Traders,** P.O. Box 27800, Tucson, AZ 85726
  - **The Nauga,** P.O. Box 2000, Mishawaka, IN 46544
  - **Heartland Products Ltd.,** Box 218, Dakota City, IA 50529.

- Never buy wool clothes or blankets again. Choose only cotton, synthetics, ramie, flannel, and other non-animal fibers. Their advantages are that they are not as likely to shrink, they usually cost less, they retain their bright colors longer, and they don't contribute to cruelty. Tell people—including store personnel—why you have gone cruelty-free. No one needs to steal from animals to be warm or to look good. Additionally, write letters protesting mulesing and live sheep exports to His Excellency Mr. F. Rawdon Dalrymple, **Embassy of Australia,** 1601 Massachusetts Avenue NW, Washington, DC 20036-2273.

- If you want warmth at the top of the world, or just in the bedroom, follow the lead of Mount Everest climbers who consistently choose Fiberfill II, Polarguard, and Thinsulate over down. These materials are more durable and washable than down, and they dry faster when wet.
- Don't buy silk products. Silk is used in cloth (including taffeta), silk-screening, and as a coloring agent in some face powders, soaps, and other cosmetics. It can cause severe allergic skin reactions, as well as systemic reactions if inhaled or ingested. Alternatives include rayon, milkweed seed-pod fibers, kapok (silky fibers from the seeds of some tropical trees), and synthetic silks.

# 35 DIAL 1-800 . . .

If liberty means anything at all, it means the right to tell people what they do not want to hear.

—George Orwell

## HELLO?

If marching for the animals isn't your style (or if a demonstration simply isn't on the day's agenda), let your fingers do the walking! Companies contributing to animal cruelty sometimes offer animal rights advocates a "free" (if unwitting!) ear in the form of their handy toll-free numbers. Designed to facilitate communication with consumers—either potential or current—800 numbers are your chance to express your feelings about crude animal tests, fur promotions, and other forms of animal exploitation directly to those who count, free of charge!

## WHAT TO DO

Here are some important toll-free numbers "for your convenience." Each 800 call costs the companies money, which reduces profits—something that often counts more to them than ethics—so the lengthier the conversation, the more impact you'll have. When you have politely griped and discussed alternatives with the usually uninformed-on-the-issue operator (or raised the blood pressure of a defensive one), ask to be transferred to another or to a supervisor. Happy chatting!

● *Companies that still test on animals:* Please ask these businesses to come into the twenty-first century and tell them you *won't* buy their products until they're cruelty free:

- **Bristol-Myers:** 1-800-448-1100
- **Clairol:** 1-800-223-5800
- **Clorox:** 1-800-677-2624
- **Cosmair** (L'Oréal and Lancôme): 1-800-462-2211
- **Johnson and Johnson:** 1-800-526-3967
- **Nina Ricci:** 1-800-245-6462
- **Noxell Corp.** (Cover Girl): 1-800-638-6204

● *Moratoriums aren't good enough:* Thank them for their progress, but tell these public-relations conscious firms that until their animal test bans are *permanent* they won't get your business:

- **Dial Corporation:** 1-800-528-0849
- **Mary Kay:** 1-800-527-3494
- **Merle Norman Cosmetics:** 1-800-421-2060

● *Major sponsors of rodeos:*

- **Adolf Coors Company:** 1-800-642-6116
- **Coca-Cola:** 1-800-GET-COKE

● *Fur promotions:*

- **American Express Fur Salon II:** 1-800-528-8000 (24 hours). Caring charge-card holders like Oakland A's Tony La Russa have become ex–American Express members because the company won't stop pushing fur. American Express' offensive inventory includes: "unplucked beaver, pastel or ranch mink with fox, dyed Tibetan lamb, reversible dyed opossum leather, Chevroned brightener added blue fox."
- **USA FOXX & FURS:** 1-800-USA-FOXX. Makes "you or your wife a QUALITY FUR GARMENT from your own untanned pelts for LESS than you dreamed possible."

- **Neiman-Marcus:** 1-800-NEIMANS
- **Saks Fifth Avenue:** 1-800-345-3454
- **Blackglama Minks/American Legends:** 1-800-445-MINK
- **Bullocks:** 1-800-284-3900
- **Robinsons:** 1-800-777-8910

- **Broadway:** 1-800-626-4800
- **Necina Fur Company:** 1-800-543-9147 (traps, too)

● *Trapping/hunting promoters:*

- **Tom Miranda:** 1-800-356-6730. Bills itself "The Trapper's Headquarters!" and sells lures, baits, books, videos, and equipment. Their selection of videos includes "new unbelievable bow scenes and lots of bears" and includes tapes such as "Professional Predator Trapping, Volume II" and "Fox and Coyote Trapping East to West: The Instructional Tape." Attempts to "increase public awareness" about trapping.
- **The Trapper & Predator Caller:** 1-800-258-0929. Subscription number for trapping magazine in which "the traditions of trapping and strategies of predator calling are covered . . . like nowhere else."
- **The Frontier Library:** 1-800-426-1357. Sells three Terry Johnson historical novels glorifying the fur trade.
- **Hoosier Trapper Supply, Inc.:** 1-800-423-9526. Traps, lures, videos.
- **Duke Traps Company:** 1-800-331-5715
- **Trappers' Special Products:** 1-800-TRAPPER
- **Ted Nugent's Wild Game Hunting:** 1-800-937-WOLF

Rock star Ted Nugent's wild game–hunting promotional line. Ted wants our nation's youths to "Whack 'em and stack 'em," and urges "getting up to your elbows in blood" as an alternative to "hanging out in the mall."

- **Arrow Walker:** 1-800-338-7389. This bowhunting advocate offers a camcorder to attach to the bow to record kills, advertised as a way to "relive the experience" by "Bringin' home the memories . . ."

● *Miscellaneous:*

- **Burger King:** 1-800-YES-1800. Protest their continued purchase of fish from Iceland (a major whale-killing country), and tell them you're waiting for a veggie-burger.
- **USDA's Meat and Poultry Hotline:** 1-800-535-4555 (Monday–Friday, 10:00 A.M.–4:00 P.M., EST). A home economist will give you an answer if you have a question about your meat or poultry products. Suggested questions: "When is this agency going to stop

promoting animal-based agriculture?'' and ''Why are male chicks allowed to suffocate to death by egg-production factories?'' Suggested comments: ''Meat tastes like chemicals'' and ''Meat makes me sick.''

• **Charles Rivers Laboratories:** 1-800-LAB-RATS. Major supplier of animals for electrode implantation and biology ''show and tell'' experiments (rats, mice, hamsters, guinea pigs) nationwide.

• **National Wildlife Federation:** 1-800-432-6564. A group whose policy statement includes this gem: ''properly regulated trapping, like hunting, poses no threat to wildlife populations, and is an indispensable research tool for scientists.''

• **Woodstream Corporation:** 1-800-233-0277. Sells backbreaker mouse-traps, fishing tackle boxes, steel-jaw leg-hold traps and other equipment.

● *Please note!* Many corporations—such as Jindo Fur Farms (''the McDonald's of fur'') and Gillette—disconnect their toll-free telephone numbers once they begin to receive calls of complaint about their treatment of animals. If this happens to any of the above, call or write **PETA** at (301) 770-7444, P.O. Box 42516, Washington, DC 20015, for current information on how to contact them.

# 36 HIDDEN HORRORS: ANIMAL INGREDIENTS AND THEIR ALTERNATIVES

At present scientists do not look for alternatives simply because they do not care enough about the animals they are using.

—PETER SINGER, *Animal Liberation*

## THE PROBLEM

Animal bits and pieces (body fats, stomach linings, and other slaughterhouse "by-products") often lurk in foods you'd never dream contained them, like cookies, flour tortillas, and roasted sunflower seeds, and in cosmetics and toiletries you smear on your face and rub in your hair! Brushes for blush and eye makeup are commonly made of hair from the inside of a cow's ear; shoe polish can contain cattle blood; and some toothpastes and cough medicines have rendered beef fat or tallow in them. Bandages, adhesives, wallpaper, sandpaper, and emory boards can contain bones, horns, and hooves. Home insulation and even the felt in felt-tip pens are made from hide and hair. Disheartening, isn't it?

## THE SOLUTION

Unfortunately, it is still virtually impossible to totally eliminate *all* cruelty inherent in our contemporary lifestyle, but the good news is that you can greatly *reduce* it by being an informed consumer.

## Become a Label Reader

Learn to identify mysterious ingredients and to question chefs, waiters,
doctors, nurses, beauticians, and others when in doubt. The following
revolting ingredients range from the obvious to the obscure, but all can
be easy to overlook:

- *Lard*. Fat from hog abdomens. Often in commercial Mexican refried beans, french fries, baked goods, and other foods. Also in
  shaving creams, soaps, and cosmetics. Alternatives: pure vegetable
  fats or oils.
- *Gelatin/gel*. Animal protein obtained from horses, cattle and hogs
  by boiling skin, tendons, ligaments, or bones with water. Used as
  a thickener for fruit gelatins and puddings, and found in many
  candies, marshmallows, cakes, ice cream, and some yogurts.
  Sometimes an ingredient in shampoos, face masks, and other cosmetics. Serves as a coating on photographic film and vitamins (and
  as medicine capsules). Alternatives: Carageen/Irish Moss, seaweeds (algin, agar-agar, kelp—used in jellies, plastics, medicine),
  pectin from fruits, dextrins, locust bean gum, and cotton gum.
- *Whey*. Milk by-product used in cakes, cookies, candies, and some
  breads and in cheese-making. Alternative: (when necessary) soy-
  bean whey.
- *Musk*. Oil painfully obtained from musk deer, beaver, muskrat,
  civet cat, and otter genitals. Wild cats are kept captive in cages
  in horrible conditions, beavers are trapped, deer are shot, and cats
  are whipped around the genitals to produce the scented oil. Used
  in perfumes. Alternatives: labdanum oil and other plants with a
  musky scent.
- *Placenta*. Afterbirth containing waste matter eliminated by the
  fetus. Widely used in skin creams, shampoos, face masks, and
  other cosmetic items; is derived from the uterus of slaughtered
  animals. Alternatives: kelp, olive oil, wheat germ oil, coconut oil,
  and other vegetable oils.
- *Collagen*. A fibrous protein in vertebrates usually derived from
  animal tissue. Used widely in cosmetics (when in doubt about its
  origin, write the company for information). Alternatives: soy protein, almond oil, amla oil, rosemary, and nettle.

- *Lactic Acid*. A slaughterhouse product, sometimes from blood and muscle tissue, produced by fermentation by certain micro-organisms. Sometimes in sauerkraut, pickles, and other food products made by bacterial fermentation. Sometimes in skin fresheners, as a preservative, and in plasticizers. Alternative: plant milk sugars.
- *Lactose*. Milk sugar of mammals. In eye lotions, foods, tablets, cosmetics, baked goods, and medicines. Alternative: plant milk sugar.
- *Other ingredients*. Keratin, lecithin, estrogen, progesterone, adrenaline, steroids/sterol, mink oil, fatty acids, insulin, mono- and diglycerides.
- **Warning:** "Natural sources," a description found on many health-food-industry labels, especially cosmetics, can mean animal *or* vegetable sources. Natural sources can include sources such as animal elastin, glands, fat, protein, and oil. Many ingredients can come from both animals and vegetable sources. If the label doesn't specify, call or write the company for more specific information.

## RESOURCE

- For a more comprehensive list, write to **PETA** for the free pamphlet, "Animal Ingredients and Their Alternatives."

# 37 | FORM A NEIGHBORHOOD ANIMAL WATCH

I could not have slept tonight if I had left that helpless little creature perish on the ground.
> —**ABRAHAM LINCOLN**'s reply to friends who chided him for delaying them by stopping to return a fledgling to her nest

If you pick up a starving dog and make him prosperous, he will not bite you. This is the principal difference between a dog and a man.
> —**MARK TWAIN**, *Puddin' head Wilson*

## THE PROBLEM

If a baby starling falls from a nest a block away, someone's beating a dog down the street, or a squirrel gets hit by a car, what happens in your neighborhood? On the heels of Neighborhood Crimespotters and Block Mothers comes **"Neighborhood Animal Watch"**—an idea first developed by caring kids and now adopted by adults in communities nationwide.

## WHAT YOU CAN DO

- Hold an evening or weekend meeting of neighbors who care about animals. Advertise in community bulletins or by hand-delivering fliers (the newspaper carrier will probably help). Learn what expertise your neighbors can add to the Neighborhood Animal Watch.

- Collect emergency and special-care numbers. Learn who to call in case of wildlife problems or if an animal turns up missing, to report cruelty, and where to borrow a trap. The printed list can be distributed door-to-door. (When you find an injured animal, call a licensed wildlife worker immediately. Do not attempt to treat injuries yourself. Always keep injured animals safe and quiet.)
- Swap information on good and bad experiences with boarding facilities, veterinarians, groomers, "pet sitters," and even dog-door suppliers. Keep a card file for neighbors' reference.
- Develop and distribute seasonal alerts (e.g., "Remember not to leave cloth bedding in dog houses in winter—it freezes when wet") and general tips (e.g., how to secure a water bucket and how to make homemade biscuits for the health-conscious dog).
- Write down license tags of unfamiliar vehicles in case they belong to "bunchers" who steal animals for labs.
- Report abuse! If you witness a cruelty in progress, contact your local humane society or humane law enforcement officer. If possible, document the abuse by keeping a journal, taking photographs, and gathering eyewitness statements.
- A colony of feral cats (domestic cats gone wild) exists (and multiplies!) in almost every community. Feeding them from time to time is helpful, but not enough. These animals or their recent ancestors probably once lived in homes and are lost or were abandoned. They are subject to disease, starvation, injury, and accident; and they need help. Borrow a humane box trap from your local animal shelter, or have neighbors chip in to purchase one from **Tomahawk Live Trapping Company** in Wisconsin, (715) 435-3550. Take the cats to the vet or the local shelter to have them examined, given the appropriate shots, and spayed/neutered—or euthanized if ill or adoption efforts fail in your neighborhood and beyond. Preventing feral cats from continuing to reproduce is the best and kindest assistance you can give them.
- When you find lost animals, your principal aim is to reunite them with their families—without alerting unscrupulous people to their plight. Most newspapers will place a free ad if you find an animal— but make your description less than thorough; the person looking for their companion should be able to describe her/him *in detail*. If no one responds, follow these guidelines: look for responsible people who want an animal to be a member of the family (not a

cheap guard dog or breeding machine); ask where the animal will live, if there are other animals in the home, and what the potential guardians feel about spaying and neutering. Always check identification. Have a signed agreement (contact **PETA** for a sample Companion Animal Adoption Agreement) that you will take the animal back if the new family cannot keep her. Don't be afraid to say "no" if you are unsure. If you are unable to find a home, take the animal to a good shelter operated by a humane organization.

## RESOURCES

- **PETA** Fact Sheets: "Guide to the Sale and Giveaway of Unwanted Animals" and "How to Trap Animals Humanely."

# 38 | SILVER SCREAM

I don't think you should hurt or kill animals just to entertain an audience. Animals should have some rights. But there are a lot of directors, including Ingmar Bergman, who will injure animals to further a plot. I will have none of it.

—The late JAMES MASON, explaining why he refused to play opposite Sophia Loren in a film containing a cock-fighting sequence.

## THE PROBLEM

Filmmakers, even in the process of portraying animals positively, are notorious for treating them as props rather than as cast members who can get tired, hot, and sick—and who are as unable to perform bionic feats as their human counterparts. Wire tripping, starvation, sleep deprivation, prodding, beatings, and "tie-downs" (whereby an invisible filament is tied around, for example, a cat to force him/her to stay in place) are methods of making an animal comply to the demands of the screenplay. Other-than-human "actors" suffer extensive physical and psychological abuse and are virtually unprotected by law. Stress, trauma, and death are, for many, the final curtain call. Some examples:

- During the filming of a stampede scene in *The Return to Snowy River: Part II,* a pregnant mare collapsed. Approximately 100 horses were used in the scene, yet no veterinarian was present. The "horsemen" could not determine what the problem was and decided to kill the mare. One struck her on the head with the blunt end of an ax, and another sliced her jugular vein. They then dumped her body into a gully. Two other horses died in the making of the film.

- In *Earth Girls Are Easy* (summer 1989), a live cat was thrown into a swimming pool, and tropical fishes were thrown on a rug to lie dying and gasping as their human counterparts joked nearby; and during the filming of *Days of Thunder* (summer 1990), seagulls were run over by beach buggies in a chase scene on Daytona Beach after being lured to the site with food.

- A spring 1990 release, *In the Blood,* glorifies "big game" hunting in a twisted homage to the late president Theodore Roosevelt. *New York Times* reviewer Janet Maslin wrote: "Not even those who object to violence will find themselves responding peaceably to this film. . . . If anything, it's enough to make audiences wish that animals had rifles, too" (April 20 1990). The film cost 31 other-than-humans their lives, the first of whom was a dozing lion who had been baited by a safari leader.

- Horses were tripped with wires in *Reds,* an ox was bled at the neck in *The Killing Fields,* and in *Apocalypse Now,* a water buffalo was macheted to death. To simulate a lion being shot in *Out of Africa,* the animal was violently pulled down by the use of a cable, according to an animal trainer who worked on the set. In *The Abyss,* rats were submerged in an oxygenated liquid and later died of pneumonia-like complications. A horse was blown up and others were tripped, injured, and killed in the 1980 film *Heaven's Gate.* In addition, an illegal cockfight was staged, and cattle and chickens were bled to get real blood to smear on actors. In *Cannibal Holocaust,* released in 1984, an opossum was slit with a knife, and a tortoise and a monkey were decapitated.

- In addition to on-screen abuse, the acquisition, care, and disposal of other-than-human "actors" raise troubling questions at a time when animal protection groups are working worldwide to protect many species from depletion due to exportation and trapping, and the complex psychological needs of other species are just beginning to be understood. Two weeks after completing the movie *Every Which Way but Loose,* Buddha (aka Clyde), the movie's celebrated orangutan "star," was found dead with blood issuing from his mouth, allegedly beaten to death by his handlers. The sworn affidavit of a worker at the compound described a session of "hitting and pounding" he witnessed one day during the filming, and other employees stated that an autopsy revealed Buddha's death was due to a cerebral hemorrhage. Orangutans are strong but otherwise naturally isolative, intelligent forest-dwellers who are happy in Borneo, not "on the set."

● Films like *Rabid*, in which frightened families resort to hideous and bizarre ways to defend themselves from animals depicted as determined to bite and kill them, can inspire or fuel irrational hatred and violent acts against dogs, bats, and other normally harmless creatures.

## THE SOLUTION

● Avoid movies that you know or suspect include real harm to animals. Write the studios responsible for such films, explaining what you found offensive, and asking for an assurance that they will portray animals positively and omit animals from their casting calls. (Excellent realistic-looking animal models exist, and it is also possible, for example, for humans to play other-than-human primates. If *Greystoke* could use human actors costumed as chimpanzees, *Project X* did not need to use real chimpanzees. The young apes should have been left with their mothers, not bothered by trainers seen on the set carrying a sawed-off pool cue, a blackjack, and a .38-caliber pistol.) Here are the addresses of major movie studios:

• **Buena Vista Pictures Dist., Inc.** (a subsidiary of Walt Disney Co.), 3900 W. Alameda Street, Burbank, CA 91505; Richard Cook, president; (818) 560-1000.

• **Columbia Pictures** (a division of Columbia Pictures Entertainment, Inc.), Columbia Plaza, Burbank, CA 91505; Dawn Steel, president; (818) 954-6000.

• **MGM/UA Communications Co.** (includes Metro-Goldwyn-Mayer and United Artists), 450 N. Roxbury Drive, Beverly Hills, CA 90210; Jeffrey C. Barbakow, president and CEO; (213) 280-6000.

- **Orion,** 711 Fifth Avenue, New York, NY 10022; Arthur B. Kim, president; (212) 956-3800.
- **Paramount,** 15 Columbus Circle, New York, NY 10023; Frank Manusco, chairman and CEO; (212) 373-8000.
- **Tri-Star Pictures** (a unit of Columbia Pictures Entertainment, Inc.), 3400 Riverside Drive, Burbank, CA 91505; Jeffrey Sagansky, president of production; (818) 972-7700.
- **20th Century-Fox Film Corp.,** P.O. Box 900, Beverly Hills, CA 90213; Barry Diller, chairman and CEO; (213) 277-2211.
- **Universal Pictures** (a division of Universal City Studios and subsidiary of MCA, Inc.), 445 Park Avenue, New York, NY 10022; Thomas Pollock, vice president of MCA, Inc., and chairman of the Motion Picture Group; (212) 759-7500.
- **The Walt Disney Co.,** 500 S. Buena Vista Street, Burbank, CA 91521; Michael D. Esner, chairman and CEO; (818) 560-1000.
- **Warner Brothers, Inc.** (a subsidiary of Warner Communications, Inc.), 4000 Warner Boulevard, Burbank, CA 91522; Robert A. Daly, chairman and CEO; (818) 954-6000.

● If you are in a movie theater and are offended at how animals are portrayed, or see a scene containing cruelty to animals, walk out! By doing so, you alert others that what happened is ethically indefensible. Let the manager know that you would not have attended if you had known there would be animal cruelty. Ask for a refund or return pass. If the explanation is firm but very polite (remember, it's not the theater's fault), most managers will be obliging and may also learn something.

● Write and ask your local movie critics to include real or perceived animal abuse in their reviews—to recognize that when a movie depicts an other-than-human being in a dangerous or uncomfortable spot, it is not always safe simply to say, "Remember, it's only a movie."

# 39 SPECIOUS SOUVENIRS

I am not basically a conservationist. When the last great whale is slaughtered, as it surely will be, the whales' suffering will be over. This is not the whales' loss, but man's. I am not concerned about the wiping out of a species—this is man's folly—I have only one concern, the suffering which we deliberately inflict upon animals whilst they live.
  —CLIVE HOLLANDS

If we are to save the world's wildlife, we must adopt an ethic that recognizes the right of all animals to exist, places equal value on the grotesque and the spectacular, and shows as much concern for the crocodile as for the cheetah, as much for the condor as the eagle.
  —LEWIS REGENSTEIN, "Animal Rights, Endangered Species and Human Survival," *In Defense of Animals,* ed. Peter Singer

What we have done to the great whales in the sacred name of commerce is an affront to human dignity, a debasement of human values and sensibility.
  In the light of present knowledge of these intelligent mammals, no civilized person can contemplate the whaling industry without revulsion and shame at the insensitivity of our own species.
  —SIR PETER SCOTT, from address to the International Whaling Commission, London, July 1979

## THE PROBLEM

The United States is the world's largest consumer of endangered and exotic animal products—followed by Japan and Western Europe. Our country's superconsumers "gobble up" products made from the teeth, feathers, shells, skins—and habitats—of species who are in immediate danger of disappearing and those who are threatened. Tourists return home with elephant-leg umbrella stands and ivory jewelry and carvings; sea turtle-shell guitars and hair ornaments, and sea turtle skin creams; Nile crocodile-skin handbags; caiman boots; python purses; and leopard-skin coats. Most exotic animal products are now illegal and can be seized, without compensation, if discovered by Customs or wildlife officials. Still, most tourists fuel the illegal market unwittingly, unable to distinguish legal from illegal animal products (not that the animals suffer more or less either way) as traders become increasingly savvy in the art of "laundering" their products from one country to another.

The World Wildlife Fund estimates that illegal wildlife trade has increased to as much as $250 million annually, from about $200 million, in less than 5 years. Such trade now ranks second only to drug trafficking among goods smuggled into the U.S. As more U.S. citizens travel to Asia, South America, and Africa, they take with them more spending money and a passion for exotic gifts.

## THE SOLUTION

- *Never* buy:

  • Ivory from elephants and from marine mammals such as whales, walruses, and narwhals, often carved into figurines, curios or jewelry. African elephants live in small herds of closely knit family groups, led by one or two older females. If (and it's a *big* "if") they survive poaching, they can reach the age of 70. The African Wildlife Foundation has estimated that 80,000 adult African elephants are killed every year for their tusks and that another 10,000 youngsters die as a result (some are killed in the process of poaching, but most starve to death).

• Tortoise-shell jewelry and combs; leather, eggs, and food products from turtles; or creams and cosmetics made with turtle flesh extract. Twenty thousand endangered sea turtles are slaughtered every year in Mexico, many as they are crawling back to sea, exhausted, after laying their eggs.

• Rugs, pelts, hunting trophies, and articles such as handbags, compacts, coats, wallets, and key cases made from the skins or furs of wild cats, including jaguars, leopards, snow leopards and tigers, ocelots, margays, and small tiger cats. Earth Island Institute reports that more than 90 percent of Nepal's fur shop coats are made from protected species. Approximately 4 rare snow leopards are killed to make coats that sell for $3,200 apiece; and it takes at least 30 "common" leopard cats to make one full-length coat.

• Marine mammal products, such as whale teeth decorated with etchings (scrimshaw) or made into figurines (netsuke), curios, and jewelry, or the furs and skins of marine mammals (sealskin toys, purses, wallets, key cases, and clothing); sea otter furs and clothing; and polar bear hunting trophies, rugs, and clothing. Scientists estimate at one time there may have been as many as 2 million blue whales, the largest animal ever to roam the planet. There are now fewer than 500. Geneticist Joseph Cummins predicts that polar bears could be extinct in fifteen years.

• Handbags and shoes made from reptile skins and leathers, particularly those from Latin America, the Caribbean, China, and Egypt. (Endangered species include: black caiman, spectacled caiman, American crocodile, Orinoco crocodile from Latin America and the Caribbean, Philippine crocodile, Chinese alligator, and Nile crocodile.) The World Wildlife Fund's list of endangered and threatened animals includes 1,200 animal species, including at least 46 varieties of turtles, 22 of crocodiles, and 24 of snakes.

• Wild bird feathers, mounted birds, and skins; and all birds, including macaws, originating in Australia, Brazil, Ecuador, Mexico, Paraguay, Venezuela, and a number of Caribbean countries. Up to 70 percent of exotic birds imported into the United States die during capture, transit, and the required 30-day quarantine.

• *Speak up!* Please, tell merchants, catalogue companies, vendors, and hotels why they should never order such goods again.

## ORGANIZATIONS

- **TRAFFIC (U.S.A.) World Wildlife Fund,** 1250 24th Street NW, Washington, DC 20037; (202) 293-4800. Monitors status of wildlife and endangered species and works to combat illegal trade. Members receive bimonthly news.
- **Friends of Animals,** P.O. Box 1244, Norwalk, CT 06956; (203) 866-5223. They state: "FOA works to reduce and eliminate the suffering inflicted by humans upon non-human animals. Our goal is to achieve a humane ethic in people's relations with the other animals of this earth." Their legislative arm does lobbying, and members receive a bimonthly magazine.
- **Earth Island Institute,** 300 Broadway, Suite 28, San Francisco, CA 94133; (415) 788-3666. An umbrella organization for a number of environmental groups. Sea turtles are their main species focus. They lobby overseas governments.
- **Division of Law Enforcement,** U.S. Fish and Wildlife Service, P.O. Box 28006, Washington, DC 20005. Responsible for monitoring endangered species trade and flow of goods into the United States.

# 40 GRIPE, GRIPE, GRIPE

The squeaky wheel gets the grease.
— ACTIVIST ADAGE

## THE PROBLEM

All kinds of organizations raffle off fur to drum up business, including cosmetics manufacturers, cigarette companies, clothiers, charities, magazines, and radio stations. Even businesses that don't seem to have anything to do with animals—such as car dealerships and hotels—can perpetuate animal abuse by keeping guard dogs in rinky-dink shelters out back or having animal heads on the walls.

Some gas stations in rural areas keep bears or other animals in cages on their lots, and a number of hotels feature caged birds or other animals as part of the "decor."

## SOLUTIONS

Whenever you see something that hurts animals or promotes their mistreatment, let management know how you feel. After all, you—the guest or patron—may be *why* the business does these things.

- Take advantage of suggestion boxes and preprinted consumer complaint cards.
- Ask shoe stores to carry a (greater) selection of non-leather foot-

wear like cloth, canvas, corduroy and synthetic shoes (e.g., Sergio Valenti).

- Ask grocery stores to stock organic produce, tofu, tempeh burgers, soy milk, Tofutti "ice cream," Fantastic Foods entrées like vegetarian chili mix and falafel, mushroom and herb pâtés by Bonavita, and Légume frozen entrées. Some grocery stores, such as the Giant chain in the mid-Atlantic states, have consumer boards that customers can apply to join.

- Complain to the manager if your apartment complex sprays its grounds with pesticides.

- Always explain your suggestions and complaints (don't just launch into a tirade of "How can you be so cruel to innocent animals?"); and always suggest an alternative. If a fur giveaway or a cruel event is imminent, try a quick telephone call, suggesting that promotions managers offer a trip or a computer instead.

- If, in your travels, you find yourself anywhere where animals are kept caged to amuse patrons, complain to the manager or proprietor while you're there and follow up your complaint with a letter when you get home. You can also report cruel conditions to the regional office of the **U.S. Department of Agriculture (USDA).** You can get the address by writing the USDA, 6505 Belcrest Road, Hyattsville, MD 20782, or calling (301) 436-7833.

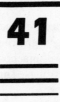

# 41 IT'S THE VEAL THING

You may love the pup-dog for his good humor, admire the fish for his face, feel like a brother to the noble horse, but no bird, beast or reptile can compare with the cow. You look into her eyes and she reads your troubles, sighs, and stops chewing her cud . . .
>    —CHARLTON OGBURN, Jr., *The Animals' Voice Magazine*,
>    February 1989

I'm somewhat shy about the brutal facts of being a carnivore. I don't like meat to look like animals. I prefer it in the form of sausages, hamburger and meat loaf, far removed from the living thing.
>    —JOHN UPDIKE, Interview for the New York Times
>    News Service, 1982

You have just dined, and however scrupulously the slaughterhouse is concealed in the graceful distance of miles, there is complicity.
>    —RALPH WALDO EMERSON, *Fate*

Has anyone sung the song of the patient, calf-bearing, milk-flowing, cud-chewing, tail-switching cow?
>    —FRANK LLOYD WRIGHT

## THE PROBLEM

Although most people who really care about animals ''gave up'' eating veal long ago, many people are deluded that other bovines frolic in sunny, grass-filled meadows until they are "humanely" killed for food. (McDonald's goes so far as to show children happy hamburgers growing on stalks in a hamburger patch!) And milk is believed to have somehow been donated by mother cows anxious to share with human beings. This is not, however, the reality for the calf's mother and father.

- Approximately 5.5 million dairy cows in the United States live in "factory" conditions, on slatted or concrete floors that cause their legs to weaken and buckle and their feet to become deformed. For months at a time they may be chained by their necks in their stalls, the milking machines brought to them. Growth hormones make their udders so heavy and swollen they sometimes drag along the ground, where teats get bruised, cut, and infected. Instead of their usual lifespan of 25 years, these gentle beings live only 3 to 5 years; most become fast-food burgers.
- "Milk cows" are fed huge doses of hormones to decrease the time between pregnancies. These hormones "beef up" flesh and can be passed on to humans through milk and meat, causing problems ranging from dysfunctional reproductive systems to premature sexual maturation.
- Cows are artificially impregnated to keep them at peak milk production, so that human beings—the only species that drinks milk beyond infancy (and not even that of our own species!)—can have their "liquid meat." Female calves are either slaughtered immediately or raised to become milk machines like their mothers. One- to two-day-old male calves are taken away from their mothers and sent to be chained by the neck inside crates in a dark building. These normally playful youngsters aren't allowed to walk or even turn around. They are fed only an anemia-inducing iron-deficient gruel so that their flesh ("veal") will be tender, pale, and non-muscular. Up to one in four calves dies in his crate. The rest stumble to the slaughterhouse truck, some so weak that they fall and break their legs.
- Cattle raised for beef are castrated, have their horns removed, and are branded without anesthetics. They are usually born in one state, fattened in another, and killed in a third. As no laws govern the trucking of "food animals," these beings suffer from extreme fear, injuries, temperature extremes (U.S. Department of Agriculture inspectors report pigs freezing to the sides of metal transport trucks

in winter), rough handling (electric shock prods, boots, and base-ball bats are commonly used to bully animals along and even to break noses), and a deficiency of food, water, and veterinary care. Millions of animals are transported daily, and cruelties are legion. When a steer falls and can't get up to be unloaded from the truck, workers have been known to tie him to the slaughterhouse dock, driving the truck out from under him.

## Did You Know

- Cattle and sheep consume 90 percent of the forage on 70 percent of all public lands in the West. The damage caused by overgrazing has brought approximately one-third of our continent's drylands into various stages of *irreversible* desertification. Altogether, the U.S. has lost approximately two-thirds of its topsoil. Eighty-five percent of this loss is attributable to livestock agriculture (87 percent of U.S. agricultural land is used for livestock production—including pasture, rangeland, and cropland).

- Many cattle eaten in the United States have been fattened up in former rain forests converted to grazing ground. Each quarter-pound fast-food hamburger of their flesh is responsible for destroying 55 square feet of rain forest. More than 50 percent of current tropical rain forest destruction is directly linked to livestock raising; and if we continue to destroy the Central American forests at the present rate, the forests will be stripped by the year 2010, causing massive damage to the ozone layer and the extinction of up to 500,000 species.

- A vegetarian world could amply support several times the current human population. For the "feed cost" of an eight-ounce steak, 45 to 50 people could each have a full cup of cooked cereal grains. Twenty pure vegetarians can be fed on the amount of land needed to feed one person consuming a meat-based diet.

- U.S. livestock eat 80 percent of the corn grown in the U.S. and 95 percent of the oats. Sixteen pounds of grain and soybeans are needed to produce one pound of feedlot beef. Whereas 20,000 pounds of potatoes can be produced on one acre of land, only 165 pounds of beef can result from the same. Sixty million people will starve to death this year; if Americans reduced their intake of meat by 10 percent, 60 million people could be adequately fed by the grain saved.

- It takes 2,500 to 6,000 gallons of water to produce a pound of meat but just 25 gallons to produce a pound of wheat. U.S. live-stock produce 20 times as much excrement as the total U.S. human population does; since feedlots do not have sewage systems, much of their waste ends up in our water.
- The most common death in the U.S. is by heart attack, for which the average American man is at a 50 percent risk. By eliminating meat, dairy products, and eggs from your diet (becoming a vegan), you reduce your risk of heart attack by 90 percent.

## WHAT YOU CAN DO

- Join the growing ranks of vegans: quit consuming cows and the milk meant for their young. A study by Dr. Takeshi Hirayama of the National Cancer Research Institute in Tokyo revealed that breast cancer rates are nearly four times as high for women who eat meat daily as for vegan women. A 21-year study done at California's Loma Linda University found that prostate cancer rates are more than three times as high for men who eat animal products as for vegan men.
- Make the transition to a diet free of meat and dairy by using substitutes, all of which are better for you, and most of which are cheaper, than cow products. Product substitutes are:

• *Meat.* In place of ground beef in tacos, chilis, spaghetti sauces, and lasagna filling, use "textured vegetable protein" (soy protein with the fat removed). An excellent TVP "Vegetarian Burger" is made by **Worthington Foods,** Worthington, OH 43085. Other substitutes include ready-made tofu and tempeh burgers, available at most health-food stores.

• *Milk.* Soy milk has become sophisticated. Edensoy, Westsoy, and other brands come in many flavors, have more character, and are lower in fat than cow's milk and are, of course, cholesterol free. They go well on cereal, steamed for cappuccino, and are equally appropriate for cooking.

• *Ice cream.* As dairy products are the leading cause of food allergies in humans and as people are abandoning dairy products for ethical reasons, a number of non-dairy frozen desserts have become available, including Tofutti (available in most major supermarkets) and Rice Dream (**Imagine Foods,** 750 Homer Avenue, Palo Alto, CA 94301; [415] 327-1444). Some supermarket chains, like Giant in the mid-Atlantic states, have their own brands of frozen tofu deserts.

• *Cheese.* Non-dairy soy cheese, such as Soymage, mimics the taste and consistency of dairy cheese; tofu can be used in vegan lasagna and cheesecake recipes (request them from **PETA**); and nutritional yeast sprinkled on tofu, broccoli, cauliflower, and popcorn provides a cheesy taste.

● Recognize meat for what it really is: the antibiotic- and pesticide-laden corpse of a tortured animal. John Harvey Kellogg, M.D., wrote: "A dead cow or sheep lying in a pasture is recognized as carrion. The same sort of a carcass dressed and hung up in a butcher's stall passes as food!"

● Join the stamina-bolstered vegetarian world of Dave Scott, 6-time Triathlon winner; Tony La Russa, Oakland Athletics manager; Edwin Moses, undefeated for 8 years in 400-meter hurdles; Paavo Nurmi, winner of 20 world records in distance running, and 9 Olympic medals; Estelle Gray and Cheryl Marek, winners of the world record for cross-country tandem cycling; and Ridgely Abele, winner of 8 national championships in karate.

● Heed the words of Dr. Neal Barnard, president of the Physicians Committee for Responsible Medicine: "We are primates, and primates are all vegetarians with only rare meat consumption by certain species. All the protein, minerals, and vitamins the human body needs are easily obtained from plant sources. The taste for meats and other fatty foods is like a substance abuse to which we are addicted early in life. While we have been struggling—and failing—to cure heart disease and cancer, their primary causes are right under our noses, on the dinner table."

# 42 SORTING GOOD TOYS FROM BAD

How would you like a big giant to come up to you and put some drops in your eyes and you couldn't touch them and just because the giant wanted to do an experiment he made you die? I think that [toy companies] should find another way to do an experiment! What good will it do to put a drop into an animal's eye, and then the animal dies? Animals (especially dogs) can help people in many ways. But then if you kill them, how can they help people?

  —**Mindi Thompson,** letter to PETA Kids, February 1990

My reading of the evidence tells me that the directiveness, the striving, of the child is toward goodness, a longing that every human being at some time in his life experiences, and that in the truly healthy human constitutes the landscape, the background of his life. What the newborn commences with by way of human nature is good. It is not neutral, or indifferent, but good—good in the sense that the child is designed to grow in the ability to love. It is human nurture that distorts and confuses.

  —**Ashley Montagu,** *Growing Young*

We must combat society's indoctrination that portrays animals as things without rights. We must make young people aware. It's surprising what they can do with the right information. They are our future.

  —**Sandy Larson,** in Karen and Michael Iacobbo's "Sandy Larson: Humane Educator," *Animals' Agenda,* May 1990

## THE PROBLEM

Unbelievably, some toy manufacturers still test their toys on animals (and no, this doesn't mean a company lets dogs carry toys around in their mouths or play tag with them!). For example, in recent tests, a toy gun that shoots capsules of paint was shot at close range into the eyes of rabbits. Not only toys themselves, but the materials that go into them are force-fed in huge quantities to rabbits and rats. Painful tests on animals do nothing to protect young consumers who risk injury when using projectile-shooting toys. For this reason, several cities, including Chicago and Milwaukee, have considered legislation to ban toy guns that really shoot projectiles.

Some toys and novelty items actually glamorize, trivialize, and even promote animal abuse. Some examples include KickDog, a stuffed toy dog for kicking when you are mad; Bad Bug, a huge, plush bee children can "smash" with a rubber mallet; Krushed Kitty, a plush half-cat toy to hang from the trunk of a car or other "kitty krushing" place; and Earl the Dead Cat, a stuffed toy promoted as "the last cat you'll ever need."

## THE SOLUTION

- Buy toys and games from companies like Kenner, Mattel, and Hasbro, that *don't* test their products on animals (you can write to **PETA** for a complete list). Choose toys that *promote* compassion for other species. **Animal Town,** P.O. Box 2002, Santa Barbara, CA 93120, 1-800-445-8642, has a mail-order catalog that includes the games "Dam Builders" and "Save the Whales." In the first, players are beavers who build dams and collect food supplies for winter while dealing with predators, including human ones; and in "Save the Whales," players work together to save marine mammals from oil spills, whaling ships, radioactive waste, and extinction.
- Protest to the following companies that have refused to commit themselves to a ban on hurting and killing animals:

• **Fisher-Price,** 636 Girard Avenue, East Aurora, NY 14052.
• **LJN Toys, Ltd.,** 3474 S. Clinton Avenue, South Plainfield, NJ 07080.
• **Spearhead Industries, Inc.,** 9971 Valley View Road, Minneapolis, MN 55344.

● Complain to the managers of any local stores carrying novelties and toys that promote animal cruelty or denigrate the dignity of other-than-human beings; and write to the manufacturers of insulting toys and games. Following are the addresses of the aforementioned cruel playthings:

• **The Murfdog Company** (KickDog), 23010 Lake Forest Drive, Suite 327, Laguna Hills, CA 92653.
• **Childswork/Childsplay** (Bad Bug), 441 N. 5th Street, Philadelphia, PA 19123.
• **Mad Dog Productions** (Earl the Dead Cat), P.O. Box 157, Richmond, VA 23201.
• **Holst/Bowen** (a distributor of Earl the Dead Cat that claims to have received only one complaint, PETA's, in the three years it has distributed this item; let them know you're out there), Room 648, Los Angeles Mart, 1933 South Broadway, Los Angeles, CA 90007.
• **Krushed Kritter Kompany of Kalifornia** (Krushed Kitty), 19528 Ventura Boulevard, Suite 328, Tarzana, CA 91356.

# 43 (GET THE) CHICKEN OUT

I think that the battery hen is the most miserable creature in the feathered world today.

—**LORD HOUGHTON OF SOWERBY,** speaking
in the House of Lords, 2 February 1981

If a robin redbreast in a cage
Puts all heaven in a rage,
How feels heaven when
Dies the billionth battery hen?

—**SPIKE MILLIGAN,** *The Animals' Voice,* February 1989

Suffering . . . no matter how multiplied . . . is always individual.

—**ANNE MORROW LINDBERG**

## THE PROBLEM

If you ever have the opportunity to get to know individual chickens, you will find—as you do with dogs, cats, and people—that some are shy, some brave, some more affectionate or outgoing than others. Each is a sensitive, feeling individual with his or her own distinct personality. Chickens make delightful, curious, and dear companions. Unfortunately, chickens are among the most maltreated and oppressed of all animals in the United States today. Like other poultry, chickens are not protected by the Animal Welfare Act or the Humane Slaughter Act.

Every year, producers for whom profits override common decency subject 5 to 6 *billion* chickens to misery that defies description.

## Did You Know

- Nowadays chickens are genetically engineered and bred specifically for egg-laying *or* for meat. Since only female chickens lay eggs, their 280 million male "layer strain" chicks per year are considered waste and thrown into plastic bags to suffocate. Sometimes the bags full of chicks are crushed by manual or automatic mallets, to be used as fertilizer or mink food.

- Female chicks are debeaked with a searing wire that, because time is money to workers, sometimes takes part of their little tongues or faces, too. Then they are placed in 12-inch-by-18-inch wire "battery" cages, with slanted wire floors, to live with 3 or 4 other hens in spaces so jam-packed (approximately the size of a record album cover) they can't even stretch a wing (the wingspan of an average leghorn chicken is 26 inches). Excrement from cages stacked above them splatters hens below. Raw sores take the place of feathers. Feet designed to walk on the earth become deformed from the slanted wire, legs become crippled, wings atrophy, and bones become so brittle that they can snap.

- A chicken is meant to live up to 20 years, but factory-farmed chickens are "used up" in 16 to 18 months, then pulled from their cages and stuffed into crates for a terrifying ride to the slaughterhouse, where they will be converted into chicken frankfurters and pot pies. There their feet are attached to a conveyor belt, and they travel upside-down, flapping to right themselves before being hit with an electrical shock that doesn't always leave them unconscious. After their throats are slit, they are dipped in scalding water. Those who survive all this, the "redskins," are tossed, still alive, into a bin to be ground into feed later.

## WHAT YOU CAN DO

- Avoid all chicken flesh and chicken "products," including eggs. (You'll be being kind to chickens *and* your health.)

- When recipes call for eggs, simply leave the eggs out or use an egg substitute, such as that made by **Ener-g Foods** (for the store nearest you carrying this product, call 1-800-331-5222). Soft or extra-soft tofu makes a great binder, as do bananas.

- If you crave the taste of chicken, explore **Loma Linda** and **Worthington** taste-alikes made of soy, available at Seventh Day Adventist food stores, many major supermarkets, and health-food stores. Some Chinese restaurants, like the Longlife Vegetarian House in Berkeley and the Harmony in Philadelphia, specialize in wheat-gluten "chicken" dishes that would fool the most discerning diner!

- Tell your family and friends the facts about chickens and eggs and help them to stop eating them. Ask restaurants to add more vegan dishes to their menus. If your local health food stores carry chickens, tell the managers that chicken flesh is far from a health food—its cholesterol content is comparable to that of beef, and its fat content is very high compared to vegetables and grains. Also, *leukosis* (chicken cancer) infects 90 percent of factory chickens and salmonellosis has been found in as many as 90 percent of federally inspected factory chickens.

- Ask your grocer to have a vegetarian line at the store so you won't have to put your groceries on a conveyor belt full of blood and salmonella leaked from packages of red meat and chicken.

- Be aware that "free-range" egg producers also kill the male hatchlings, and few let "spent" hens retire in their old age.

- Broaden your eating horizons both in ethnic restaurants, that specialize in savory animal-free dishes, and with new recipes in your own kitchen.

- Alert others by writing letters to editors to protest the cruel treatment of chickens in this country.

- Ask your congressional representatives to introduce bills for better treatment of chickens, and for the outlawing of the *battery cage* (a wire cage the size of an album cover in which 4 chickens are commonly kept at a time).

- Insist on vegan meals in school and office cafeterias. Contact the **Physicians Committee for Responsible Medicine,** P.O. Box 6332, Washington, DC 20015, for recipes that are especially formulated for institutions.

# 44 GIFT TABOOS AND GIFT "TO-DO'S"

So, my Christmas present was a fur coat. I froze. How could I show gratitude or pleasure when all I could think of was the ugly way in which those twenty or so foxes must have lost their lives?

—MARYBETH TODD

## BACKGROUND

When shopping for humans, give other-than-humans a gift, too—by checking your list to make sure your choices aren't naughty but are nice to *all* animals! By exercising your consumer clout, you can refuse to help cruel businesses and corporations continue to profit from animal suffering. You'll get a feeling of satisfaction knowing that every dollar you spend on products from animal-friendly companies helps them grow and expand. Your gifts will also send a positive message to your friends and family.

## TABOOS

- You wouldn't want your friends to look like prehistoric cave dwellers, would you? So steer clear of fur, leather, wool, down, silk, and animal skins when you are gift shopping. With all the humane alternatives available, there's no excuse for the ruthless slaughter of animals.
- If cosmetics or perfume are on a friend's wish list, hit the cosmetics giants still testing on animals where it counts: at the cosmetics

counter. Don't buy—and tell the vendors and producers *why* you won't buy—products made by companies still testing on other-than-human beings, like Guerlain (which uses pig fat in its processing!), Calvin Klein, and Lancôme. Instead, choose Christian Dior's "Dior," Elizabeth Taylor's "Passion" (but beware, some bottles come in a mink pouch), Benetton's "Colours," and perfume by Yardley of London.

- Exercise a strong will and apply careful thought to battle the temptation to give an animal as a gift. Only give such a gift if you are *absolutely certain* that the recipient has met and wants this particular companion animal (not one who just looks similar or has the same coloring); has the time and physical and financial ability to care for him or her properly (veterinary care is expensive); and understands and can accept the enormous responsibility and life-long commitment to the animal. Then, get the animal from the pound, not the pet shop.

## TO-DO'S

- For those who love to cook, a subscription to *Vegetarian Times* (P.O. Box 570, Oak Park, IL 60303) is twelve gifts in one. Each issue is full of informative articles and enticing recipes. There are also dozens of vegetarian cookbooks available that are sure to please tastebuds everywhere, or give a cook a chance to get out of the kitchen with a gift certificate to a vegetarian restaurant.
- Introduce others to cruelty-free living with a decorative basket full of bath, hair, and other personal-care products available from The Body Shop and at Caswell-Massey stores. The Body Shop has oodles of exotic products—from Japanese washing grains to charming pig-shaped nailbrushes to seaweed and birch shampoo. Caswell-Massey stores are stocked with delightful fragrances for men, women, and the home, as well as all sorts of skin- and hair-care products. Both stores offer gift certificates. Your friends will be overwhelmed by the hundreds of wonderful products to choose from! They'll want to spend hours sniffing at The Body Shop's perfume bar, where they mix fabulous scents together to create their own one-of-a-kind signature fragrance. Write to **The Body Shop** at 45 Horsehill Road, Cedar Knolls, NJ 07927-2003 and to

**Caswell-Massey** at 111 Eighth Avenue, New York, NY 10011 for store locations and to order catalogues.

- The Nature Company stores provide plenty of fabulous gift ideas, including beautiful prints and posters, relaxing musical recordings, colorful mobiles, books, and much more. Call **The Nature Company** at 1-800-227-1114 for locations and ordering information.

- **PETA** can provide lists of toy companies that don't test on animals so that you can be sure the toys you give are safe, fun, *and* humane. (Talk about mixed messages: Barbie's profile claims that she's an animal rights activist but also says she works at McDonald's!) Stuffed toy animals (especially those that talk) are sure to be a hit for the kids on your list. Just watch out for real fur!

- A birdbath or feeder, or a squirrel feeder or nesting box, will invite bushy-tailed or winged acrobats whose antics are sure to provide endless amusement.

- Make a vegetarian gift basket—or have your local fancy food store (like Maryland's **Sutton Place Gourmet**) or health-food store (like Washington, DC's **"Yes!"**) construct one for you. Load it with mushroom paté, wild rice pilaf, spicy bean dip, canned gazpacho, falafel and Barat tofu chocolates.

- Give a cotton shipping basket, cotton espadrilles, or a cotton-covered, cedar-chip dog bed.

- Give **Sierra Club** diaries, **World Wildlife Fund** calendars, and other beautiful prints and notecards from environmental and animal protection organizations. Patronize **Greenpeace** stores in San Francisco and Washington, DC.

- Give flower or vegetable seeds, a window box, a sprouting kit, a lilac bush, an herb garden, an organic vegetable gardening magazine subscription, or copies of Helen and Scott Nearing's books *Living the Good Life* and *Continuing the Good Life*.

# 45 | LOBSTER TALES

Poor animals! How jealously they guard their pathetic bodies . . . that which to us is merely an evening's meal, but to them is life itself.

—T. Casey Brennan

They really are very interesting little creatures. And to look into those eyes and to know that's a hundred million years of history—it's incredible.

—Cam MacQueen, lobster liberator

Don't eat anything with a face.

—Animal Rights Maxim

## THE PROBLEM

What if grocery stores kept live dogs (or even commonly consumed cows) crammed in filthy glass containers with their legs taped together, and what if accompanying recipes suggested dropping the fully conscious animals into a pot of boiling water? People would be outraged. But swap the mammalian victims for those with claws and antennae, and who cries of "injustice!"?

## Crustacean Revelation

- Lobsters are fascinating. They have a long childhood and an awkward adolescence. They use complicated signals to explore and establish social relationships with others. Their communications are direct and sophisticated. They flirt. Their pregnancies last 9 months. Some are right-handed, some left-handed. They've even been seen walking hand-in-hand! Some can live to be more than 150 years old, though few (1 percent) survive the world's most devastating predator—the species with whom lobsters share so many traits—the human being.

- Like us, lobsters are vertebrates who feel pain; when they are tossed into scalding water, their claws scrape the sides of the pot as they struggle to get out. Their frantic and fruitless efforts have caused more than a kitchenful of cooks pangs of guilt.

- Crustaceans are sensitive creatures who possess a will to live and who struggle as best they can against death. Knowing lobsters and crabs feel pain, we shouldn't allow prejudice to dictate to our palates and consciences.

- "University of Maine researchers say that 'ghost traps' (traps lost on the sea or bay floor) are keeping many lobsters trapped for months and sometimes even years. Lobsters can survive indefinitely in the lost and abandoned traps because enough food passes through to keep them alive. A new law requires that all wire lobster traps be equipped with a biodegradable escape panel that opens after a period of time" (*Animals' Voice Magazine*, Vol. 6, No. 2).

## WHAT YOU CAN DO

- Eliminate lobsters, crabs, and other sea animals from your diet. There are plenty of reasons not to eat them, including bacterial contamination and seafood poisoning (lobsters eat sewage from processing-plant runoff). Your body, designed to digest a flesh-free diet, will thank you for avoiding an unnecessary strain.

- Tell your waiter to hold the butter *and* the lobster. In restaurants, voice your objection to their live lobster tank and follow up with a letter of complaint. Point out that these nocturnal creatures deserve better than to exist on display in crowded tanks twenty-four hours a day. Let them know that you look forward to eating there again when the tank is removed and that you will be encouraging your friends, family, and co-workers to boycott as well.

- Write letters of complaint to supermarkets that sell live lobsters. A Colorado Springs woman delivered information on lobsters and the cruelty of live displays and cooking methods to a grocery store manager. She was thrilled to learn later that the store would no longer sell live lobsters because "some lady raised a huge ruckus."

- Watch out for lobster tanks at airports. Stop, preferably when someone is considering a purchase, and discuss your feelings about lobsters.

- Some specialty stores will ship live lobsters to the customer "on ice." Make sure that any catalogues you receive that offer such shipments get a letter of complaint, preferably in their postage-paid envelope.

# 46 THE SHOW MUST *NOT* GO ON

The wild, cruel beast is not behind the bars of the cage. He is in front of it.

—AXEL MUNTHE

## THE PROBLEM

Circuses, rodeos, and other acts that feature animals may draw cheers from the audience but they are no fun for the animals. Show sponsors force them to "give up" their natural lives and swap the forest, oceans, and jungles for life in travel trailers, small tanks, or cages. The animals are trained to perform repetitious, puzzling (to them), grossly uncomfortable, dangerous, and frightening acts, such as standing on their heads or jumping through hoops of fire (instinctively feared by most animals).

- In circuses, bears are kept in neck chains and muzzles, elephants stay shackled by the leg when off-stage, and big cats have their claws removed. All quickly learn to fear the whip, the hood, and the electric prod. Former animal-act trainers admit that electric prods, food deprivation, and beatings are common training "techniques."
- "Wrestling" bears and "diving" mules are often an attraction at county fairs, shopping malls, bars, and carnivals. Wrestling bears often have their claws and teeth surgically extracted and can be drugged to prevent injury to the humans who challenge them. Diving mules can be zapped with electric prods until they are

"conditioned" to plunge head-first into a pool of water from a 30-foot-high plank.

- Traveling shows subject animals, even pregnant ones, to journeys of hundreds of miles in poorly ventilated railway boxcars and trucks. Carnival-act animals may never leave their trailer cages, see sunlight, feel the ground, or experience the touch or companionship of another animal.

- On their way to the slaughterhouse, some cattle are compelled to suffer one last gig at the rodeo. In the assorted "events," steers and calves are kicked, prodded, stung with electric "hot shots" and various caustic substances, and jerked to the ground by a neck rope at speeds of up to 27 miles an hour. A flank or "bucking" strap is tightly pinched around their abdomens and causes the otherwise nonviolent animals to buck. Some animals are dragged away from the arena, suffering from torn ligaments, broken bones, and other injuries, and then sent on to the slaughter.

- Zoos may at first seem harmless, but a closer look shows us that animals imprisoned there are usually bored, neurotic, and far, far from home. At places such as the so-called "IQ Zoos," a rabbit in a glass box "plays" the piano and a chicken may "dance" (is she being electrically shocked?). At petting zoos, lion cubs and other animals are sometimes tugged and pulled at by over-eager children.

- A big round of boos goes to events such as alligator wrestling and greased pig contests, in which the animals are not only chased but thrown and dragged around by their hind legs and ears. Commonly misunderstood or *feared* animals like these are often treated in ways that would be unanimously condemned if the victims were those more attractive or familiar to us. Ignorance of species' interests and individuals' needs does not justify subjecting any animals to a life of taunting, confinement, and abusive handling.

## WHAT YOU CAN DO

- Boycott *all* animal acts and exhibits.
- Make every effort to ensure that traveling animal acts take a detour past your town. Take your message to the sponsors (store owners and managers and radio and television stations). Inform promoters

about the problems with animal acts and urge them to withdraw their support. Don't assume that sponsors won't care about animal suffering—it's safer to assume they aren't informed. Ask them to reconsider their support, and urge them not to repeat sponsorship the next time the show comes to town.

- If sponsors ignore your request, arm yourself with signed petitions and take your concerns to your city council. Contact your local humane society to encourage them to get involved. As proof that such efforts pay off, the city of Hollywood, Florida, passed legislation banning all animal acts and exhibits. (Hooray for Hollywood!) Make a compassionate case to your local legislature and urge them to show your county's (or better yet, your state's) respect for animal life by passing a similar ordinance.

- If the show is booked in spite of your efforts, be on the scene with picket signs and leaflets. Dressed in a clown, cowboy or other appropriate costume and with a friendly smile, you're sure to reach many people.

- Educate the group that animal acts try to appeal to most: children. Most children have a natural affinity for *all* living beings and are upset when (*and if*) they learn about cruelty to animals. Take them to see shows whose entertainment value comes from amusing and unusual human performances—rather than pathetic other-than-human acts. Non-animal circuses include the *Cirque du Soleil* (a miracle of choreography and costumery) and the Pickle Family Circus (a wonderfully imaginative circus).

- Put on your canvas hiking boots and observe animals' *natural* behaviors on *their* turf instead of behind glass and steel or in silly costumes.

- Finally, rainy-day activists and less adventurous types can learn from *National Geographic* specials, travel videos, and zoology/ nature books, as well as from visits to the local nature center or by subscribing to wildlife protection organizations.

# 47

# TIME OUT: CHOOSE ANIMAL RIGHTS, NOT ANIMAL "SIGHTS"

For what do the good people see who go to the gardens on a half-holiday afternoon to poke their umbrellas at a blinking eagle-owl, or to throw dog-biscuits down the expansive throat of a hippopotamus? Not wild beasts or birds certainly, for there never have been or can be such in the best of all possible menageries, but merely the outer semblances and *simulacra* of the denizens of forest and prairie—poor spiritless remnants of what were formerly wild animals.

—HENRY S. SALT, *Animals' Rights*

The thinking [person] must oppose all cruel customs no matter how deeply rooted in tradition and surrounded by a halo. When we have a choice, we must avoid bringing torment and injury into the life of another . . .

—ALBERT SCHWEITZER

## THE PROBLEM

Competing for tourists' dollars with "exciting" and "different" attractions, vacation establishments sometimes "resort" to unwitting cruelty, especially in the form of supposed cultural highlights. Hotels, touring companies, individual entrepreneurs, and even local governments sponsor or create attractions like wild animal parks, bird shows, bullfights, and photo opportunities with lion cubs, infant monkeys, or others. Vacationers are lured to these attractions intending only to soak up the local color and enjoy a pleasant experience.

- Although horse-drawn carriages may seem romantic and innocent, they have been banned in several cities, including Paris, France; Las Vegas, Nevada; Palm Beach, Florida; and Santa Fe, New Mexico—while bills seeking bans are pending in many other areas. The horses can work up to 16 hours a day without rest and with little or no food or water (to avoid unsightly excretion while they work). With their noses at car tailpipe level, they breathe exhaust fumes that, over the long term, cause respiratory infections. Some collapse and die of exhaustion in the heat, as the pavement temperatures are usually 20 degrees higher than the ambient temperature. "Carriage horse operations are a threat to humans as well as to horses," says Cam MacQueen of the Maryland-based Coalition to Ban Carriage Horses. "Horses are naturally timid and flee when alarmed. If a car backfires, a horse surrounded by automobiles, bicycles, and pedestrians has nowhere to run except into traffic. It happens."

- Perhaps the most notorious tourist attraction is the bullfight, a spectacle so offensive that 90 percent of those who attend one never return. No fair challenge, it is a fight between bulls who are debilitated and tormented beforehand and "brave" matadors who will face little danger. Vaseline is smeared into the bulls' eyes to blur their vision, their horns are filed blunt, irritants are rubbed on their legs to throw them off balance, and cotton is stuffed up their nostrils to shorten their breath. In so-called "bloodless bullfights," the only type that is legal in the United States, the bulls survive the public torment only to be slaughtered immediately afterward.

- Hotels and restaurants often use live animals for "decoration" or in shows. Birds, lions, tigers, primates, alligators, fishes, and other "exotic" animals are subjected to a (usually abbreviated) lifetime of confinement, boredom, and loneliness. Las Vegas show animals are often on public view day and night while "between shows." The Westin Hotel in Kauai, Hawaii, is one example of a resort in which the luxury is for humans only: myna birds are confined in a narrow wrought-iron cage within sight of the great outdoors; a baby kangaroo and other imported animals live as curiosities on tiny artificial "islands," and "retired" cart horses from the mainland ferry guests to and from the beach.

- Don't forget cockfighting. Though banned in all states except Ar-

izona, New Mexico, Oklahoma, Louisiana, and Missouri, cock-
fights continue illegally throughout the U.S., especially in the
South, as well as legally in Central and South American countries.

## WHAT YOU CAN DO

● *Don't be taken for a ride.*

• If you see horse-drawn carriages in any city, please write your
objections to the local paper, the chamber of commerce, the board
of trade, and the mayor. If the carriage-horse operation is affiliated
with a hotel, tell the manager, too.

● *Speak out.*

• The vacation industry depends on your money and recommendations to stay in business. Make hotel management and owners
aware that animal cruelty does not "amuse" or "entertain" you
and that you won't return to the hotel until the animals have gone.
• Report back to your travel agent, letting him/her know that wit-
nessing animal exploitation spoiled your vacation. Suggest that the
agency choose another hotel to recommend to clients.

● *Fight the bullfight.*

• If you're traveling to Mexico, Spain, or Italy, help spare the
pain of the 30,000 bulls who are killed in the arena each year.
Don't attend bullfights, encourage others not to patronize them,
and avoid purchasing souvenirs that depict any aspect of bullfighting.
• Write to **PETA** to receive free leaflets in Spanish and English
to distribute at your hotel and in the airport.
• Protest "bloodless bullfights" if they appear in your city (within
the past few years, this spectacle has occurred in Chicago, Illinois;
Phoenix, Arizona; Houston, Texas; Artesia, California; and Dodge
City, Kansas). Write your objections to local papers and legislators.

● *Cock-a-doodle "don't."*

• If you see evidence of illegal cockfighting, call the police. If
you live in a state in which cockfighting is legal (see above), write
letters to legislators and local papers.

# 48 | ADVERTISING ACTION

Let us dare to read, think, speak and write.
—JOHN ADAMS, second president of the United States

## THE PROBLEM

While relaxing in front of the television set or flipping through a magazine, we see lots of attractive animals, from bulldogs to monkeys, featured in advertisements or "posing" or "acting" in a show. Our first reaction is usually "Aw, isn't s/he cute." But a second look should make us concerned about how those animals felt being painted, crammed into motorcycle helmets, or worse.

- Abuse can be as subtle as forcing a cat to stay awake for hours in order to be able to sleep "on cue," or as obvious as being hit on the head with a blackjack or spun in a washing machine. Penguins have been dressed up and stuck under bright studio lights until they collapsed from the heat.
- **The American Federation of Television and Radio Artists (AFTRA),** 260 Madison Avenue, New York, NY 10016, acknowledged such abuses when it unanimously passed a resolution in 1989 calling for its members to report any act of cruelty to the nearest AFTRA office. Stating that "the occurrence of animal abuse on union sets is becoming more and more apparent," the federation resolved that "no performer should be expected to work on a set where an animal is being subjected to abuse."

## THE SOLUTION

We don't have to sit back passively—we can let producers know we want them to write animals *out* of their scripts and tell advertisers that their use of fur wraps, rodeo cowboys, and orangutans smacking their lips turn us *away* from, rather than *towards* the beer, cars and other products they want us to buy.

- Keep a stack of blank, prestamped postcards by your television viewing chair. Whenever you see any animal doing something awkward, confusing, dangerous, or demeaning—or a wild animal doing *anything*—write a polite "opinion note" to the show's producer (in care of the network). Here are the addresses of the major networks:

  - **ABC,** 1330 Avenue of the Americas, New York, NY 10019
  - **CBS,** 51 W. 52nd Street, New York, NY 10019
  - **NBC,** 30 Rockefeller Plaza, New York, NY 10020
  - **PBS,** 475 L'Enfant Plaza, Washington, DC 20004
  - **CNN,** One CNN Center, Atlanta, GA 20248
  - **FOX,** 10201 W. Pico, Los Angeles, CA 90035

- Call local television stations during shows misusing animals to express your concern and let them know why you changed channels.
- Encourage pro-animal and anti-cruelty themes by dropping notes of thanks to the shows using them. (They'll certainly hear from the other side.) Positive reinforcement can make a difference during their next creative session.
- Take the postpaid subscription cards out of magazines that accept advertisements in which animals appear to be demeaned or abused, put your comments on them, and mail them back in.
- Let manufacturers know that their products won't be in your shopping cart until their company has a policy *not* to use performing animals in its advertisements. Creative advertising is great, but compassionate creativity is greater!
- If you work for an advertising agency, educate your colleagues. Implement a policy, like those of Ads Unlimited in New York and Chase, Pickett, and Putscher Associates in Illinois, banning the

use of animals by your agency—or try to get such a policy adopted.

- Type short, one- or two-paragraph letters to the editors of magazines that run ads showing animal abuse. Also, write producers of shows in which characters wear fur or in other ways demean or injure animals (see below).

## Sample Notes

To the Editor:

I am very distressed to see [company name] using tigers to sell deodorant in your magazine. Tigers belong in the jungle, not in the studio. Animals used in advertisements are all too often abused in training, shipment, acquisition, and even disposal.

Until these advertisements are halted, I will not buy from [company name]. Animals are individuals with interests of their own, not merchandising tools. Please refuse to run ads like this.

Dear Producer,

I love [program title] and was so sorry to see [its star] in what appeared to be a lynx coat last [day of the week]. [Star's character] is surely not supposed to be so shallow and uncaring as to patronize the slaughter of these magnificent cats. The other characters' failure to criticize the coat as less than glamorous seems out of touch with current public opinion against cruelty to animals in the fur trade.

Your response would be appreciated.

# 49 | DONATION DO'S AND DON'TS

Charity is indivisible. If a man resents practical sympathy being bestowed on animals on the ground that all ought to be reserved for the species to which he himself happens to belong, he must have a mind the size of a pin's head.

—**C. W. HUME,** *The Status of Animals*

## BACKGROUND

Private philanthropy is a vital component of our society; it bears much of the weight of coping with vast social and health problems, pulling up the slack for a government increasingly unwilling to fund desperately needed services. Charity organizations and foundations that provide voices for the voiceless and succor for the needy require our support, but we must watch where donations go, no matter how prestigious the organization.

## BE INFORMED

- The American Cancer Society devotes only a fraction of its research budget to tracking *human* cancers and has been accused of ignoring environmental carcinogens (probably the single greatest cause of cancer) while it funds tens of thousands of dollars worth of experiments on living animals each year and cancer remains our country's number 2 killer.

179

- The American Heart Association has spent many thousands annually on experiments in which monkeys, dogs, cats, and other animals are repeatedly starved, shocked, immersed in water, subjected to extreme temperatures, and physically restrained, sometimes for months on end—"proving" that stress affects the heart adversely.
- Remember, quite a few "environmental" and "wildlife" organizations support hunting, trapping, and/or fishing. The Sierra Club, the World Wildlife Fund, the National Audubon Society, and the National Wildlife Federation are among them.
- Some professional fund-raisers send direct-mail appeals and sweepstakes offers for cancer and animal rescue work that takes only the tiniest fraction of their budget; the rest goes into their pockets. Ask around, and don't hesitate to ask for budget breakdowns and *verification* of any publicized good works, not just good words.

## BEFORE YOU GIVE

- Ask exactly what your money will fund. If it includes experiments on animals, write on the contribution form: "I will resume contributions when you discontinue animal experiments"—and return it *without* a donation. If you feel you must support a particular medical charity, request that your money not be used for research on animals—and require confirmation to that effect.
- Ask to review an annual report. Look beyond self-promotion for evidence of *tangible* programs and gauges of success, such as numbers of indigent patients treated, numbers of wheelchairs, walkers, or hearing aids distributed, numbers of acres preserved, numbers of books or films donated to schools, or numbers of animals sterilized.
- Tell pro-hunting charities that you respect the "life" in "wildlife," and that the environment "belongs" to other-than-human beings, too.
- Charities that raise funds by raffling fur or other items taken from animals, or that sponsor exploitative events such as rodeos or circuses with animals, need to know why that makes you a *former* donor.

- Remember that your local shelters (for homeless beings of any species), hospices, and other *direct-care* facilities need your help— both hands-on and financial.
- Support organizations like the **American Fund for Alternatives to Animal Research (AFAAR),** at 175 W. 12th Street, Apt. 16G, New York, NY 10011, whose innovative programs do much good without hurting others.

# 50 SIGN ME UP!

The combined force of a few thousand sparks makes a powerful bolt of lightning.

—ARLO GUTHRIE

It takes only one person to change your life—you.

—RUTH CASEY

## WHAT NOW?

Now that you have a basic grasp of things you can do individually, it's time to network into the animal rights community—to be part of the big picture. What follows is a list of various animal protection organizations—some generalists, some very focused. It isn't meant to be comprehensive—there are thousands of good groups—but it's designed to give you an idea of the types of specialized national organizations that are out there and need your support of their work for animal rights. Check locally too, especially if you have time and/or talent to donate. Undoubtedly, you will find lots of groups whose goals and tactics feel comfortable and right to you.

*The Animal Organizations and Services Directory* (Animal Stories, 3004 Maple Avenue, Manhattan Beach, CA 90266; $24.95) is a comprehensive guidebook profiling over 550 organizations. Includes national, state, and professional organizations; hot-lines; animal behaviorists; clubs and associations; periodicals; and much more.

## Multi-Issue

- **Animal Welfare Institute:** P.O. Box 3650, Washington, DC 20007; (202) 337-2333. Concerns include: humane treatment of laboratory animals and the development and use of non-animal testing wherever possible; the preservation of species threatened by extinction; reform of cruel methods of trapping wild animals; prevention of cruel experiments on animals by untrained youths; and reform of cruel methods of raising food animals. Books, films, pamphlets. Membership: $15 regular; $5 student. Members receive AWI quarterly.

- **Argus Archives:** 228 East 49th Street, New York, NY 10017; (212) 355-6140. Maintains active files on over 850 organizations in the U.S. and abroad, including publications of those organizations. Collects books, magazines, and clippings on issues involving animal suffering. Individuals may consult archives by appointment. Argus issues well-researched publications, including bibliographies and indexes.

- **The Fund for Animals:** 200 West 57th Street, New York, NY 10019; (212) 246-2096 or 246-2632 (office) or (212) 245-4430 (hotline). Uses resources to protect both domestic and wild animals and fight animal cruelty wherever it occurs. Projects include: saving hundreds of starving horses by relocating them to the Black Beauty Ranch; working to stop hunting; fighting to save the wild horses and burros; and many other animal abuse causes involving the rescue of animals. Membership: $15 adult; $10 student; $25 family. Members receive magazine twice yearly.

- **People for the Ethical Treatment of Animals (PETA):** P.O. Box 42516, Washington, DC 20015; (301) 770-7444 (office) or (301) 770-8980 (Action Line). The largest animal rights organization in America. Motto: ''Animals are not ours to eat, wear, or experiment on.'' Encourages the humane treatment of animals; exploring non-animal testing methods; opening up laboratories for public scrutiny and research accountability; improving legislation governing the humane treatment of animals; establishing public outreach/ education campaigns, e.g., vegetarian and fur campaigns. PETA's Research and Investigations Department is largely responsible for closing down the largest horse slaughterhouse operation in the

U.S.; the first and only conviction of an animal experimenter in the U.S.; and the first confiscation of abused laboratory animals under court order. And PETA's Caring Consumer campaign successfully pressured industry giants like Avon, Benetton, and Estée Lauder to stop animal testing. It has many resources, including fact sheets and brochures, case reports, cruelty-free shopping guides, bi-monthly *PETA News* magazine. Large merchandise catalogue includes books, T-shirts, bumperstickers, activism manual, cruelty-free household products and videos for purchase or loan. Membership: $15 regular; $3 PETA Kids.

## Cultural Activism

- **Culture and Animals Foundation:** 3509 Eden Croft Drive, Raleigh, NC 27612; (919) 782-3739. Committed to fostering the growth of intellectual and artistic endeavors that are united by their concerns for animals. Funds three programs: (1) scholarly research into the concern for animals; (2) original work by artists that expresses positive concern for animals; and (3) performance and presentation of intellectual and artistic work that is compatible with its aims. Videos and films available. Membership: $25 individual; $15 student/senior; $40 family. Members receive news of activities throughout the year and may purchase materials at discount prices.
- **National Society of Musicians for Animals:** 61 Hedgely Road, Springfield, OH 45506; (513) 322-1624. "NSMA is a network of pro-animal musicians, whose primary purpose is to educate, entertain and inspire the public in behalf of animals and environmental issues, and to further an ethic of compassion and nonviolence."

## Lab Animal Protection

- **American Fund for Alternatives to Animal Research (AFAAR):** c/o Dr. Ethel Thurston, 175 West 12th Street, Suite 16G, New York, NY 10011-8275; (212) 989-8073. Bestows grants to develop non-animal substitutes for tests; publishes findings of research in reports to agencies, interested scientists, and others; demonstrates that certain experiments on living animals are harmful to humans or unnecessary; and informs people of the cruelty in animal experimentation. Affiliated with **International Association Against Painful Experiments on Animals (IAAPEA)**. Funded solely by contributions.

- **Health Care Consumers' Network (HCCN):** c/o Lawrence Carter, P.O. Box 6322, Washington, DC 20015; (202) 686-2210. HCCN was formed to be a voice for people whose lives have been affected by serious illness but choose not to be used as excuses for cruel animal experiments—instead, demanding a say in how research is conducted. Funded solely with contributions; contributors receive regular Action Alerts. Members are medical care recipients and their families.

- **Last Chance for Animals:** 18653 Ventura Blvd, Suite 356, Tarzana, CA 91356; (818) 760-2075 (office) or (818) 760-8340 (hotline). Anti-vivisection, direct action animal rights organization dedicated to the eradication of animal exploitation. "Our direct action philosophy is modeled on the philosophies of Henry David Thoreau, Gandhi and Martin Luther King, Jr." Maintain twenty-four-hour recorded information hotline regarding demonstrations and fundraisers.

- **National Association of Nurses Against Vivisection (NANAV):** P.O. Box 42110, Washington, DC 20015; (202) 770-8968. Unites members of the nursing profession who wish to challenge the myth that the use of animals in research is necessary and to promote a more effective allocation of our limited health resources by emphasizing prevention, including a vegetarian diet. Membership (open only to registered nurses, licensed practical nurses and nursing students): $15 regular; $10 student. Annual NANAV newsletter.

- **New England Anti-Vivisection Society (NEAVS):** 333 Washington Street, Suite 850, Boston, MA 02108; (617) 523-6020. The society's goal is the abolition of animal experimentation. NEAVS works to accomplish its goal through public education, legislative change, and the development of alternatives to live animal research. On the federal level, NEAVS is responsible for the "standing" bill (H.R. 2345) which would allow individuals and organizations to bring suits against the USDA for failure to enforce the Animal Welfare Act. NEAVS takes its four-part education program "Students Think About Animal Rights" to public schools and sponsors an annual essay contest. Available: pamphlets, books, bumper stickers, and buttons. Membership: $10 individual; $5 student/senior; $250 life. Members receive the *Members Quarterly* magazine and periodical newsletters.

- **Physicians Committee for Responsible Medicine (PCRM):** P.O. Box 6322, Washington, DC 20015; (202) 686-2210. Promote alternatives to animal experiments; promote preventive medicine through nutrition programs; consumer group concerned with better health care; parent organization of HCCN. Materials available: nutritional information, recipes, disease prevention information. Membership: $20 regular; $10 medical students.
- **Psychologists for the Ethical Treatment of Animals (PsyETA):** P.O. Box 87, New Gloucester, ME 04260; (207) 926-4817. An independent association of psychologists dedicated to the promotion of animal welfare within the science and profession of psychology. Primary objective is to lessen the suffering of animals in laboratory, educational, and therapeutic settings. Available: "Humane Innovations and Alternatives in Animal Experimentation." Membership (any person with an advanced degree in psychology or degree in progress): $20 full member; $10 student. Members receive the "PsyETA Bulletin" twice yearly.

## Religion and Animals

- **International Network for Religion and Animals:** 2913 Woodstock Avenue, Silver Spring, MD 20910; (301) 565-9132. Objective: to bring religious principles to bear upon humanity's attitude toward the treatment of nonhuman animals. INRA is ecumenical and international in its outreach. Membership: $15 regular; $10 student/senior; members receive a newsletter and discounted prices on all resource materials.
- **Unitarian Universalists for Ethical Treatment of Animals:** 230 W. 78th Street, New York, NY 10024; (212) 724-3842. UFETA works with over one thousand congregations to introduce the issue of animal rights and to initiate observances on church calendars (Meat-Out Day, World Day for Animals in Laboratories, World Prayer Week for Animals, etc.); encourages congregations nation-

wide to adopt resolutions for the rights of animals and incorporate the philosophy and language into sermons; sponsors a major animal rights speaker every June at the General Assembly to address the over five thousand attendees who are mostly religious educators, ministers, etc. Membership: $15 supporting; $25 sustaining; $40 organization. Contributors receive a newsletter twice a year in addition to several other mailings.

## Politics, Legislation, Litigation

- **Animal Legal Defense Fund (ALDF):** 1363 Lincoln Avenue, San Rafael, CA 94901; (415) 459-0885. Comprised of attorneys who bring lawsuits to establish the rights of animals and work to establish laws for animal rights. As these lawyers are interested in changing the laws instead of reaching quick settlements, potential "clients" should also be willing to devote time and some costs to follow the lawsuit through to its completion. Contributors receive a quarterly newsletter.
- **National Alliance for Animal Legislation:** P.O. Box 75116, Washington, DC 20013; (703) 684-0654. National grass-roots organization dedicated to promoting humane legislation. The alliance pursues this goal by lobbying at congressional hearings, providing analysis of bills, monitoring congressional support for humane and progressive legislation, and holding educational workshops. Membership: $25 regular. Members receive quarterly *Capitol Hill Report,* Action Alerts, and a congressional report card showing how our federal representatives support or fail to support bills concerning animals.

## International

- **Concern for Helping Animals in Israel (CHAI):** P.O. Box 3341, Alexandria, VA 22302; (703) 533-8366. Helps the Israeli animal welfare community expand and modernize the existing animal shelters in Israel and builds shelters where there are none; provides needed veterinary equipment and supplies; provides funds to enable the shelters to hire personnel to routinely inspect the condition of animals used by food vendors; makes humane education materials available; and sponsors contests in the schools to promote positive attitudes in Israeli children towards animals. Available: videos, books, buttons, T-shirts, and notecards. Membership: $10 individual; $18 family; $50 supporter. Members receive the *CHAI Lights* newsletter two times per year plus updates two times per year.

- **World Society for the Protection of Animals:** 29 Perkins Street, P.O. Box 190, Boston, MA 02130; (617) 522-7000. Coordinates international effort to promote effective means for the protection of animals. Membership: $20 individual; $40 family. Members receive "Animals International," a quarterly newsletter, and updates on on-going projects.

## Marine Life

- **The Cousteau Society:** 930 West 21st Street, Norfolk, VA 23517; (804) 627-1144. Primarily an environmental education organization dedicated to the protection and improvement of the quality of all life. The society produces television films, conducts research, delivers lectures, publishes books, and issues other publications. Also available: calendar, posters/prints, t-shirts, videos, sculptures (write for an order form). Membership: $20 individual; $28 family. Members receive the bimonthly full-color "Calypso Log" and two-color newsletter *Calypso Dispatch* seven times a year.
- **Earth Island Institute:** 300 Broadway, Suite 28, San Francisco, CA 94133; (415) 788-3666. Initiates and supports internationally oriented action projects for the protection and restoration of the environment; identifies crucial and emerging public action; builds networks among international constituencies. Program includes action projects, Earth Island Centers, and the *Earth Island Journal*. Available: T-shirts, posters, books, jewelry, and videos. Membership: $25 regular; $15 student/low income; $50 contributing. Members receive the quarterly "Earth Island Journal," project updates and a 10 percent discount on merchandise.
- **Sea Shepherd Conservation Society:** P.O. Box 7000-S, Redondo Beach, CA 90277; (213) 373-6979. Money contributed is used to run the "Sea Shepherd," a marine mammal protection, conser-

vation, and research ship. Crew is made up of volunteers and represents several nations. Ship used to confront whaling vessels and shut down the Canadian harp seal hunt in 1983, saving an estimated 77,000 seal pups. Actions have also been taken to halt the slaughter of dolphins by Japanese fishermen. Contributors receive the quarterly newsletter.

## Anti-Hunting

- **Committee to Abolish Sport Hunting:** P.O. Box 43, White Plains, New York, NY 10605; (914) 428-7523. Works to abolish all forms of recreational hunting through a program of public education and legal challenges and through debate by representing the anti-hunting view in the print media and on radio and television. Membership: $20 annual. Contributors receive the committee's Bulletin and/or Action Alert when appropriate.
- **The Fund for Animals:** (see above, "Multi-Issue").

## Horses

- **American Horse Protection Association:** 1000 29th Street N.W., Suite T-100, Washington, DC 20007; (202) 965-0500. Dedicated entirely to the welfare of horses and other equine animals, wild and domestic. Principal purposes: to preserve and protect wild, free-roaming horses and burros, to prevent abuse of horses in competition, to assist state and local animal welfare organizations and concerned individuals to solve problems of neglected and mistreated horses, to promote safe and humane transportation of horses, and to educate the public in proper and humane horse care. Staffed almost entirely by volunteers who fight for humane treatment of horses through litigation, investigation, and public awareness. Contributors receive a quarterly two-color newsletter.

## Primates

- **International Primate Protection League:** P.O. Box 766, Summerville, SC 29484; (803) 871-2280. In countries where primates live, IPPL's field representatives (in Australia, Bangladesh, Brazil, Canada, Ghana, Hong Kong, South Africa, Pakistan, Vietnam, India, and many more countries) work to create and preserve national parks and sanctuaries, and for the strict regulation of primate hunting, trapping, and sale. IPPL's educational efforts have contributed to decisions by many countries to ban or restrict primate trade and establish programs to protect primate habitats. In the importing countries, IPPL works to monitor all primate trade. Members also monitor the conditions of zoo and laboratory primates in their localities. Available: T-shirts. Membership: $10 regular; $7 student; $25 sustaining. Members receive a subscription to the quarterly *IPPL Newsletter,* which features in-depth analysis of primate problems, an annual report on sanctuary gibbons, and action alerts.
- **Primarily Primates Sanctuary:** P.O. Box 15306, San Antonio, TX 78212-8506; (512) 755-8868 or (512) 755-4616. A sanctuary and rehabilitation center for over three hundred primates, exotic birds, small mammals, and reptiles who have come from abusive or negligent situations, from the pet trade, labs, zoos, and the entertainment industry. Provides native habitats and rehabilitation for species to socialize with their own kind and develop natural instincts in a safe environment—with the hope of someday returning them to their native habitat. Contributors receive a newsletter three to four times a year.

## Greyhounds

- **Greyhound Friends:** 167 Saddle Hill Road, Hopkinton, MA 01748; (508) 435-5969. Objective: to place retired racing greyhounds in appropriate adoptive homes and monitor their progress. Places an average of five dogs per week. Available: T-shirts/sweatshirts, and postcards. Contributors receive notices of events and pertinent legislation.

## Animal Rights

- **Association of Veterinarians for Animal Rights (AVAR):** P.O. Box 6269, Vacaville, CA 95696; (707) 451-1391. Provides testimony on animal-related legislation and at government hearings; is involved with integrating ethical perspectives concerning the use of animals into the teaching of veterinary medicine; provides a forum for like-minded veterinarians to discuss their concerns on the issues. Available: books and films. Membership: $30 veterinarians; $10 veterinary medical students; $20 supporting. Members receive a bimonthly newsletter *Directions,* action/legislation alerts, and may request a position statement.
- **Feminists for Animal Rights:** P.O. Box 10017, North Berkeley Station, Berkeley, CA 94709; (415) 547-7251. Group of feminist, vegetarian women dedicated to ending all forms of animal abuse. "Since exploitation of animals and women derives from the same patriarchal mentality, our struggle is for women as well." Distribute feminist and animal rights information on an international basis. Available: books, buttons, T-shirts, rubber stamps, and cassette tapes.

## Vegetarianism

- **EarthSave:** 706 Frederick Street, Santa Cruz, CA 95062; (408) 423-4069. A nonprofit environmental, educational organization informing people about the cumulative impact of America's food choices. Shows people how our food choices affect our health, happiness, and the future of life on earth. Membership: $20 regular; $15 students/seniors; $35 family. Members receive a quarterly newsletter and a 10 percent discount on merchandise.
- **Physicians Committee for Responsible Medicine (PCRM):** (see above, "Lab Animal Protection"). PCRM's *Guide to Healthy Eating* has six issues a year; the subscription rate is $12.95 (for PCRM members $9.95). The guide is full of beautiful food photographs, and each issue comes with ready-to-use recipe cards. Attention doctors and nutritionists: You can now order "The Guide to Healthy Eating" in quantity at a special reduced price. Every

two months you will receive multiple copies of the current issue, which fit right in the display rack included, at no extra charge. Your patients will appreciate your giving them the vital information they need. Call or write for current rates.

- **The Vegetarian Resource Group:** P.O. Box 1463, Baltimore, MD 21203; (301) 366-VEGE. A nonprofit group working on both local and national levels to educate anyone interested in any aspect of vegetarianism. Membership: $18 single; $25 family; $10 low-income. Members receive *Vegetarian Journal*.
- **Vegetarian Times:** P.O. Box 570, Oak Park, IL 60303; (708) 848-8100. A comprehensive source of information about vegetarianism. Provides answers to questions about health and nutrition, recipes and other vegetarian-related issues.


## Factory Farming

- **Humane Farming Association:** 1550 California Street, Suite 6, San Francisco, CA 94109; (415) 771-CALF. HFA members (including public health specialists, veterinarians, consumer advocates, family farmers, humane societies, and others) are united in a campaign to eliminate the severe and senseless suffering of animals in factory farms. Currently spearheading the National Veal Boycott, a campaign to ban battery cages, and a national television and magazine advertising campaign against factory farming. Available: posters, factory farming photographs, literature, videos, and more. Membership: $15 annual. Members receive *HFA Watchdog*, bulletins, and action alerts regarding legislation and demonstrations.